My
Father's
Stash

My Father's Stash

Escaping the World of Secrets, Shame, and Guilt

*"I was instantly changed in a profound moment of curiosity
and discovery. Little did I know what lay ahead.."*

Jerry D. Wright

TATE PUBLISHING
AND ENTERPRISES, LLC

Published by Tate Publishing & Enterprises, LLC
127 E. Trade Center Terrace | Mustang, Oklahoma 73064 USA
1.888.361.9473 | www.tatepublishing.com

Tate Publishing is committed to excellence in the publishing industry. The company reflects the philosophy established by the founders, based on Psalm 68:11,
"The Lord gave the word and great was the company of those who published it."

Published in the United States of America

ISBN: 978-1-62295-301-1
1. Self-Help / Addiction
2. Self-Help / Spiritual
12.12.14

Dedication

I dedicate this book to the many friends in my life who have accepted and loved me in spite of my many faults. Among those are the many men who have participated in men's accountability groups over the years. My pastor, staff, and the dedicated godly leadership of my church have also stood firmly with me as I have shared my story with others.

I dedicate this to my two beautiful daughters and my son-in-law who have shown me love and support throughout my journey to sobriety. I am sharing my story for the future of my four grandchildren with the hope and prayer that you will choose a healthier path than your grandpa chose in his younger years.

Lastly and most importantly, I dedicate this book to my lovely bride of thirty-eight years, Kathy. You have reflected the love of Jesus Christ to me more than anyone I have ever known. You are the one I love the most. You have my heart forever. You chose to stay with me in spite of my utter stupidity. You stayed with me in spite of the rotten choices I made in the midst of my addiction. I am forever grateful to you for continuing to love me. It is a privilege and honor to be called your husband, lover, and friend. I am the most blessed man on earth. As our grandkids say with so much honest and sincere affection, "I love you with all my heart!"

CONTENTS

FOREWORD

I've heard a variation on the story a thousand times. "I was ten years old and I found a discarded magazine down by the creek." "I was nine years old and I found some videotapes in the barn." "I was eleven years old and I was looking through my dad's dresser and…"

My friend John Mandeville called me late one night in 1998 and said, "If I don't tell someone my secret I'm going to lose everything." His secret was an addiction to Internet pornography. The barn example above was John's story.

John's reaching out to me began a journey that is still going on fourteen years later. I soon learned that John was only one of seven men in my circle of friends who were living this double-life nightmare. And those were just the ones I knew about.

Seven years researching and interviewing dozens of men and their wives resulted in me producing "Somebody's Daughter," a DVD/CD set to help set men free from pornography.

Then this past year while in Oklahoma City I heard of an organization called Men Living Up and was told

I had to meet its founder. I had the privilege of meeting Jerry Wright a few days later. Within a few minutes I knew I was talking to a very special guy.

Jerry is instantly likeable. I guess you'd call him a man's man. He's big and strong with a firm handshake and a warm smile and outgoing personality. He puts you immediately at ease. And then he tells you his story.

If you're reading this book, it's probably a story not unlike your own. It's the story of a young boy, with a natural curiosity about the opposite sex, introduced to images beyond his ability to process—images that seared themselves into his mind and released a wash of chemicals over his brain that laid the foundation for years of struggle.

After finding freedom from that struggle, Jerry felt a calling to help other men and their families find the victory and restoration that he had experienced in his own life and marriage. He especially felt called to take his message to the church—a place where, unfortunately, too many men have struggled in silence and shame for far too long.

You are holding the result of that calling in your hands.

In this book you will find information that will help you understand why pornography has been a problem for you. You will hear stories of other men like yourself and realize that you are not alone.

Perhaps most importantly, you will be given concrete steps that will begin to set you on your own path to personal victory and freedom from pornography use.

It took courage for you to pick up this book. I pray that in these pages you will find the hope you need to turn your life around. You've beaten yourself up mentally over and over because of your pornography use. But now, by reading this book, you are taking a constructive step towards breaking the cycle of guilt and shame.

That first exposure to pornography doesn't have to be your destiny. Jerry Wright is proof of that. Let his story motivate and inspire you!

You're taking the first steps toward becoming the man that God has called you to be. And you can get there. You can be free.

May God bless you as you walk that path to freedom.

— Steve Siler
Director, Music for the Soul
Producers of Somebody's Daughter:
A Journey to Freedom from Pornography
August 2012

PREFACE

My Father's Stash is the result of my lifetime of challenge, frustration, shame, guilt, fear, and finally, victory. I have spent many years in recovery learning about how I tumbled into the secret world of addiction. As I started my recovery, I started learning as much as I could about sexual addiction. I spent countless hours reading, studying, and journaling. The more I researched, the more I realized that there are many commonalities in the stories of sex addicts. Early exposure to pornography is a huge factor, as well as links to a family history of addiction.

The medical and psychological fields are slowly catching up to the science of sexual addiction. As of this writing however, the Diagnostic and Statistical Manual of Mental Disorders does not recognize Internet addiction, gambling, sex addiction, or pornography addiction as clinical addictions.

If you are one of the people who have been, or currently are, involved in addictive behaviors, you know how difficult it is to quit your behaviors. I hope to educate you on some of the reasons why it is so hard to stop as well as provide hope for ending your pattern of shame and guilt.

While I address my story from my own personal perspective as a man, women are also falling prey to many of the same issues in today's culture. From one youth pastor:

> We have tried to address pornography addiction, but are finding parents will not allow us to discuss this topic. I am finding more and more of our young ladies are dealing with pornography and sexual sins...but their mothers are getting in the way. This is a tough issue to address!

I hope and pray that *My Father's Stash* will encourage, strengthen, and motivate you to examine yourself, seek help, stop the behavior, and ask the questions that will lead you, or someone you know, to recovery.

INTRODUCTION

After talking to hundreds of men, I have discovered a brotherhood of men who share some of the same elements of my story. Not every man develops a lack of control regarding lust. Many men grow up nurtured by their parents, are well-educated, and properly informed regarding healthy human sexuality. Many men are raised in a loving home. Many more men have not been taught anything at all about healthy human sexuality. *Flying by the seat of your pants* is the norm. Learning *on the street* is silently expected and encouraged.

My Father's Stash could just as easily have been named, *My Brother's Stash* or *My Neighbor's Stash* or *The Stash My Mother Gave Me* or *The Stash I Found in the Dumpster*. It seems every man is introduced to pornography in a different way. It doesn't matter how you were introduced, if you were introduced at a young age, you have probably struggled with controlling or stopping your viewing of pornography. If you were introduced to pornography in the Internet age, you have had nonstop access to pornography most of your life. I pray that you have been strong enough to resist the urges that are so ingrained in testosterone-filled males. Many of us have not.

With the increase of Internet use and its proliferation, thousands—and perhaps millions—of men are finding themselves trapped by the twenty-four-hours-a-day, seven-days-a-week smorgasbord of sexually explicit Web sites. Primetime and family time television are rapidly becoming equally provocative. The envelope is being stretched as to what is acceptable and protected by first amendment rights.

The growing level of exposure to sexual erotica is being met with silence. Christian men and women are being drawn into the trap; along with the rest of society, their voices are silenced because they are trapped too. Churches are silent, because a great number of clergy are trapped along with their flocks.

My Father's Stash is my attempt to share my real-life story, a story of someone who has fought the battle, learned a great deal about addiction, and now wants to share the knowledge gained along the way.

As I have talked to hundreds of men, there never seems to be enough time to talk about all of the facets of this addiction. It seems I always leave something out. *My Father's Stash* provides a comprehensive, while not fully complete, guide to overcoming the power of sexual addiction. This book is a starting point for many men and pastors. *My Father's Stash* won't fix you. Only God and a repentant heart will lead you to complete healing. For women reading this book, I pray that it will educate you about the difficulty of the long-term struggle for the man in your life. For many men, it's not as simple as *just stop doing it.*

Some may find my comments controversial. Others will find them to be *right on the mark.* It will depend on your perspective, background, and the environment you came from. I ask you to keep an open mind and withhold judgment until you read the entire book.

Sexual temptation is everywhere in today's American society. I offer some help and encouragement, as well as some practical tools, to help you fight the battle and win.

I pray that God will give you the strength and guts to start the journey. It won't be easy. As a matter of fact, it can be one of the greatest challenges you have ever faced. In spite of the challenge, isn't it time to start?

Finding my Father's Stash

This journey started for me at a very young age. To say my family was dysfunctional would be like saying dogs hate cats. We were obviously messed up. It was obvious to my three sisters and me, but no one else knew what was happening behind closed doors. My father was a hardcore, abusive, and mean alcoholic. There was both physical and mental abuse, mostly directed toward my mother. I received my share of abuse and learned very early on how to protect my inner self. In the middle of one of my dad's tirades, I remember saying to myself, "I'm not going to let you in." This, of course, created many relationship problems as an adult. I wouldn't understand the full impact until years later.

With the daily and weekly stress, any escape was a welcome way to deal with my sadness, loneliness, and despair. My introduction to pornography was at the young age of nine. I discovered my dad's porn stash on a shelf in his closet. If he was trying to hide it, he didn't do a very good job. I can still remember the colors in the room. I can still remember the texture of the paper and how thick the stack of magazines was. Every detail, including those first images I saw as I flipped the pages, is as clear in my mind now as if I had seen them thirty seconds ago.

Having no experience with anything sexual, I was curious and intent on seeing as much of this new, exciting material as I could. I knew instinctively that this was something I would have to do secretly. This became my escape from the sad feelings and loneliness that I had endured for so long. Looking at the magazines made me somehow feel different... better. It was an escape. Like the secret that our family *had problems*, this was my secret, but instead of making me depressed and angry, it made me feel good, at least initially. Little did I know that my brain was being transformed by these images of naked women. The wiring of my brain was being reprogrammed. I didn't know that pornography has been compared to cocaine addiction because of similar neuro-chemical activity in the brain. I was in the early stages of preparing my body, mind, and soul for a lifelong addiction to pornography.

As time went by, I had periods of time where I really wasn't very active in trying to find these images. It seemed every time I would make "headway," one of my friends or classmates would break out their stash of porn. Once, in high school, an assistant coach took several guys by his house on the way to a game. He proudly pointed out his porn magazines sitting boldly on his living room coffee table. That wiring in my brain that I had spent hours developing would, each time, strongly pull me back in. Porn does not become an addiction for every man, but the younger a male is exposed to pornography, the more likely he is to become addicted.

My interest in girls, other than porn women, began in sixth grade. Because of the false portrayals I had seen in magazines, I had no idea what a true relationship with a girl should look like. I didn't have a model of a good relationship at home, and of course sex was never discussed. Like most guys, I learned *on the street*. As most guys will admit, this is not the best way to learn. I had a few girlfriends through high school, but I was not able to develop any deeply connected relationships.

I was very good at hiding my inner conflicts and my addiction. On the outside I was a pretty normal kid, but on the inside I was in deep despair about why I couldn't stop my consistent habit. This was a topic no other guys would dare mention. It seemed all the guys wanted to do was brag about their sexual exploits or attempts with girls. I had no idea that many of my male friends and classmates were struggling with the same issues.

I eventually met my sweetheart and future wife in high school. I thought that marriage would finally satisfy my constant urges and sexual desires. After all, we could have all of the sex we ever wanted. Things went well for a while and then it became obvious that we had different ideas about the frequency and kind of sex that was mutually satisfying. My expectations were those I had seen and observed while viewing pornography. Her expectations were of closeness, romance, and tenderness. She was always wanting to talk and talk and talk. I wanted to *get right down to business.* I had it figured out in my mind: God made man and woman to be together; He gave us the matching parts to make it all work, so why not just jump in and enjoy each other! After a few months and years had gone by, it was glaringly obvious to me that she was *messed up.* She had no idea what a man wants and needs. It was easy, with my history, to turn to porn once again. Again, I was an expert at hiding it and trying my best to act normal (As if I knew what normal was). At home I simply tried to avoid conflict with my wife. I just desired *peace* with her, not intimacy.

At this point, let me say that I became a Christian at the age of thirteen. Many times after becoming a Christian, I had prayed, begging God to forgive me and take these urges away. I would vow to never look at porn again, only to fail time after time. It seemed that God would give me peace for a very short time, but then I would return to my old habits, often times acting out in even more intense and dangerous sexual activities. It was a cycle I could see and feel, but I wasn't ready to deal with it. I enjoyed it, and I thought it brought me happiness and pleasure. The truth, however, was that I was totally isolated on an island by myself... alone. I frequently thought, "There has to be something wrong with me. Why can't I stop?"

After many, many years of secret sexual gratification, I finally hit a point of complete and utter frustration. I was completely depressed and angry with myself for not being able to overcome this problem. I finally began the process of trying to understand what was wrong with me. I knew that this *inner conflict* was going to destroy me. I wanted answers, but I didn't know where to turn. Just like in the general society, sex and sexual addiction were never discussed in church. If it were, the most frequent comment would be, "Boy, the preacher handled that pretty well." Then it would not be discussed again for years, if at all. It was as if the preachers would say to themselves, "Well, we covered that subject, let's move on." Only after my recovery started did I learn that addiction to pornography is just as prevalent in churches as it is in society. I would have never thought that a preacher—a man of God—could be looking at porn. Surely, the seminaries were screening and training preachers about the dangers of pornography.

My first day of recovery was at a marriage seminar that my wife and I attended. We had already been to a half dozen seminars over our long marriage. In the past I was simply trying to appease my wife. I attended this one with a different attitude in my heart. I had reached a point in my life where I was tired of *living a lie*. I was tired of the cycle of highs and lows. I was tired of not having a deep, intimate relationship with my wife. I wanted to change *me*.

For a few months before the seminar, I had been pleading with God to give me the opportunity to share my struggles with my wife. I was ready to accept the consequences for my moral failures. I was willing to endure my family's disappointment and rejection. I was willing to sacrifice everything to *end the shame*. During one breakout session, the leaders had each couple leave the seminar, go to lunch, and urged each couple to share something that they had never shared before. Wow, what a Holy Spirit moment! My heart was pounding in my throat. I decided right then and there that I was going to tell my wife my deep, dark secret. At lunch, sitting in a drive-in restaurant, I spilled my guts to my wife. Let me stop right here and give a warning to any guys who might be reading this and are considering telling their wife they are addicted to pornography. It might be best to share with your clergy or a professional counselor first.

This was the most painful, hurtful, and disappointing moment in my wife's life. I felt better *dumping* all of this garbage on her, but she was absolutely destroyed. We spent many, many weeks and months following this moment, working through the pain I had caused her. I had betrayed her. I had replaced her with total strangers who were willing to take their clothes off and do *despicable* things in a fantasy world. The hurt will never completely go away. The trust she had in me before this was destroyed. I have to earn her trust back everyday. She is a loving, caring, and accepting partner with me now, and I am so grateful that she has chosen to stand by my side in spite of my weak and flawed human condition.

Besides my unbelievable wife, the person who has stood by me the most has been my pastor. When I said I was willing to change *me*, I was serious. The day after I shared with my wife, I went to see my pastor. I hadn't known him long, but I had served with him for two years as an elder. Can you believe someone *serving* in a church leadership position could have this problem? I was ready to resign my volunteer church position and leave the church. As soon as I finished my story and history and admitted my addiction, he had a few simple words to say to me.

He said, "I love you, and there is nothing that will ever stop me from loving you. There is nothing that will ever stop God from loving you. You can serve here as long as you feel God is asking you to."

I was in utter shock and total disbelief—no judgment, no condemnation, just love? All of my life in church, I had heard the message of unconditional love, but now—for the first time in my life—here was a man demonstrating it toward me. I was blown away!

It has been a long, difficult road since then. I'm not going to candy-coat this fight. It is by far the toughest thing I have ever done. The major challenge was that the God-given desire to look at a beautiful woman seems to never go away. I can choose to control my eyes, but every glance is a step in the wrong direction. The other challenge is that temptation is everywhere in today's world.

Each day presents challenges and obstacles: magazine covers in convenience stores, scantily clad women on television, and women who wear skimpy, low-cut outfits to name just a few. Women who think they are dressing attractively and fashionably are unknowingly causing men to stumble. For those ladies reading this, I know what you're thinking: "If men would just control themselves…" I'm not blaming women for dressing attractively. God created women to be beautiful and attractive to men. Women were also created to fill many other important, God-pleasing roles apart from men. If you remember the Bible story in Genesis, Adam and Eve were made to be the perfect pair. In their perfection, they were naked and not ashamed. Only after *the fall* did they require modest clothing. I'm sure Adam thought Eve still looked pretty *hot* in her "garments of skin" provided by God. Somehow I don't think it was the low-cut, see-through, leopard-spotted nightie that men fantasize their wives wearing.

I see men differently now. Like me, most men tend to be on an island by themselves. Men are not as open to deep, personal dialogue as women. Most men don't have someone to talk to about the issues with which they struggle. Many women have no clue about these issues. The most common response I get from women when they hear stories of men's struggles is, "I had no idea," or denial: "I'm so glad my husband is not like that."

I catch myself watching men's behavior more closely now, too. I'm keenly aware of men's eyes drinking in the hot babe who walks by in a miniskirt. I see them linger at the magazine rack and stop at the bikini-clad beauty, open the pages, and feast. For me, it's now an opportunity to remember how I used to be filled with uncontrolled passions and desires. I don't walk down the magazine aisles anymore. I also now have an understanding, willing partner who knows to *check me* at the shopping mall, or to switch seats with me at a restaurant when a provocatively dressed woman sits in my line of sight.

The struggle with lust continues to be a day-by-day, hour-by-hour journey for me. My hope and prayer is that my story will help others find the courage and strength to end the shame. Finding out that I was not alone was both encouraging and helpful to me.

We will win this long-term struggle one man at a time. Society will change one father and one family at a time. Isn't it time to *draw a line in the sand?* The next generation of men is looking to you right now.

My family history also played a major role in my falling into temptation.

MY FAMILY HISTORY

My father passed away on May 29, 2011. He was a broken man and very fragile at his death. The last week of his life, the family had called hospice in to help with his final care.

I spent most of his final seven days visiting and talking with him. He was alert and coherent until his death. The final two and a half days were some of the best days of my life. Dad and I talked and talked and talked. We no longer felt the need to carry on the typical, superficial father-son conversations we had had so many times in the past. You have to understand that I had a lot of anger and resentment toward my father. Growing up, I absolutely hated my father. He had made life miserable, chaotic, and downright dangerous for everyone who occupied his home.

Now at the end of his life, I felt pity. I was so sad for him that he had wasted so much of his life, dealing with his own addictions and pain. For as long as I can remember, my dad drank. He wasn't just your ordinary, casual drinker. When dad started drinking, he would continue until he would reach the point of being unconscious. Dad was also a mean drunk. He would fight anyone who crossed his path, most often with no reason or provocation. He would fight the neighbors who occasionally tried to calm him down in one of his many weekend binges.

On these last two days of his life, my dad and I talked about his family history and what he had experienced as a child. He had never talked much about his childhood or his father. I knew that my father was one of twelve children from a mixed family. His family was dirt poor. He was raised in the depression and lived on a farm. The family consisted of eleven boys and one girl. Wow, can you imagine the challenges for his one sister? She's the oldest and has outlived all of her brothers. She is one tough lady.

As we talked, I began asking my dad about his father. I never knew my grandfather on my dad's side of the family. He died before I was born. My dad had never shared any details about his relationship with his father. My dad started telling me that his mother became ill when he was eighteen to twenty-four months old. Since his mother could not take care of a small, infant child, my father's uncle and aunt volunteered to take him to live with them in Texas. His uncle and aunt had another son, an only child. Not only had my father been separated from his family, he was also treated like a stepson in his new home in Texas. My father wound up living with them until he was eleven years old.

My father described how he would get to visit his family once a year and stay for a week. When it was time for him to go back to Texas, he recalled hiding in the fields, because he didn't want to leave his family again. On one occasion, my father recounted how he had heard his father telling his mother that he wanted him to move back with the family. Overhearing the conversation, my father heard his mother say she didn't want him to come back. My heart ached for my father as he described the hurt and pain it had caused him to hear that his mother didn't want him. She had never bonded with her son. With twelve children and struggling to feed them everyday, I cannot imagine the stress and worry that my grandparents endured. In spite of very difficult circumstances, how could someone reject one of their own children?

I told my father that he had done nothing wrong. He had simply been at an age where his mother couldn't take care of him. She didn't pick him out of a line. She didn't choose him to punish. He was simply chosen because he was an infant boy who needed constant care and attention. My dad lay in his bed, staring at the ceiling as a tear slowly ran down his cheek. I began to understand some of the underlying pain that had caused my father to want to numb his feelings through the use of alcohol and later, pain medications. Instead of talking about his feelings of rejection and his hurt, he simply medicated himself with alcohol; feeling emotional pain was simply unbearable for him.

Was there a link between my father's alcoholism and drug addiction and my sex addiction? My father also described to me how his father had told all eleven boys as they reached puberty to "make as many women as you can." In today's language, "have sex with as many women as you can." What a terrible statement to make to your sons. What kind of impact did this have on my father's ten brothers? I know most of his brothers were also alcoholics. Several of his brothers were well-known *womanizers*. Does this give an insight into my grandfather's past? I think it clearly demonstrates the dysfunction and lack of healthy teaching that was passed from generation-to-generation.

I have committed my life to breaking this chain of addiction, chaos, and dysfunction for my family and the generations that follow after me. I know of no greater role for a husband, father, and grandfather. To break the chain of addiction, someone has to start talking about addiction in his or her family. With God's help, I plan on being the first link in a new chain of healthy sobriety.

DAD IS
FINALLY HOME

My father's health had been failing for the last ten years. He had two failed back surgeries and suffered severe chronic pain. As I've said, in his earlier adult years, he was an alcoholic and suffered from severe depression. In the last ten years, he had become addicted to prescription pain medications. He also began taking increasing amounts of depression and anxiety medications. Due to the amounts and variety of medications, my father suffered from periodic bouts of bowel obstruction. This is what eventually led to his body and organs shutting down.

In May 2011, my father fell at his assisted living center. A few days later, he complained about pain on his right side, so I took him to the emergency room to be examined. He was diagnosed with another bowel obstruction. This time there was nothing the doctors or hospital could do. His bowels had simply turned into a gelatin mass.

I met with my mother and sisters to talk about what we should do. Six months prior to this, I had experienced hospice care with my father-in-law. We decided to call a hospice organization to consult with the family. My father was coherent and fully aware of the gravity of the situation. My family chose to use the same hospice company and the same caseworker that had cared for my father-in-law. After hospice talked to the entire family, including my father, arrangements were made to transfer him to a nursing home just a few miles from my home. He was transferred on Friday afternoon. Once his medications for pain were balanced to manage his pain, the family was encouraged to fulfill their own family duties. On Sunday evening at 8:00 p.m., I was contacted by the hospice nurse. She said that my father's time was very close. I quickly left a family gathering and contacted my sisters and my mother. It took forty-five minutes to arrive at the nursing home. One of my sisters had arrived just a few minutes before me. My father had just passed away prior to me entering the room. I cried and hugged my sister who was also crying. I gently closed my father's eyes as the nurses verified that he had died. I immediately called my oldest sister, who was bringing our mother to the nursing home, and told her that our father had just died. Just like my father-in-law, at the time of death, my father appeared to be at complete peace.

I had always been fearful to be around death and dying. I remember, as a child, the fear and dread of going to extended family member's funerals. I did not want any part of death. I did not understand the cycle of life or the fact that one could be gone at a young age or an old age. Life seemed to be never ending.

As a Christian, I don't fear death. I know I don't understand everything about death fully, so there will always be a twinge of uncertainty in my mind about death. Doubts are a part of human nature. It's normal to question things that cannot be seen or fully understood.

Mostly, I fear leaving behind the ones I love. At death, have I given enough of myself to my family and friends? Have I done something of value that will make a difference in someone else's life? Have I changed the world in some small way that will give God more glory? These are the questions that facing death causes me to ask.

In my experience with death, I felt an overwhelming sense of thanksgiving. My father's life was a frustrating and painful existence in his latter days and years. The joys of life and living had been replaced with frustration, disappointment, disease, and a longing for something better. While I am extremely sad at my father's passing, I am also grateful that he has been taken to a better place and freed from the prison of his broken body.

The existence of God and His promises was confirmed to me through my father's death. On October 3, 2003, while on a mission trip to Southeast Asia, I had a dream or vision about my father. It was the most vivid and real dream I have ever had. In this dream, my sister and I were sitting at a picnic table on the west side of our church. It was a beautiful, sunny day. Somehow I knew that this was the day of my father's funeral. In the dream, our father started walking toward us. Since our father was such an abusive alcoholic, this caused my sister and me to have great anxiety and fear. We weren't sure what was going to happen. As my father approached us, I noticed that he looked different. He appeared to be about thirty to thirty-five years of age. He was standing erect; he was slim, muscular, and quite handsome. His skin was tanned, appearing almost burned. He had a glow about him. Arriving at the picnic table, my dad starting apologizing for the kind of father he had been to us. After he had spoken a few words, I jumped up and wrapped my arms around him and started talking to him about the love and forgiveness of God. At this point, he placed his hand on my shoulder and said, "Jerry, it's going to be okay. God has changed me." With these words, I woke up. It was the middle of the night in Southeast Asia. I immediately grabbed my journal and began writing everything down that I could recall about this dream.

My father wasn't a Christian at that time. I wasn't sure that he would ever become a Christian, but I knew that God had given me a promise that he would become a Christian. In 2006, on a Saturday morning, I had a choice of either going to work or going to see my mother and father at their home. I felt compelled to go see my mother and father. When I arrived, my father was by himself.

My father had always struggled with faith and trusting God's promises. I don't remember what caused the conversation to turn spiritual, but it did. We talked about what God said in the Bible about becoming a

Christian. I shared with my father the dream I had been given in Southeast Asia a few short years earlier.

I asked my father if he had ever prayed and asked Jesus to come into his heart and be his best friend forever. My father told me, "Jerry, I don't know how to pray." That day, at the age of seventy-seven, my father prayed to God and became a Christian.

Two weeks before my father's death, I was leaving a men's Bible study group on a Tuesday morning. As one of my friends and I were in the lobby, I looked out across the church parking lot. On the west side of the church was a picnic table. There had never been one there before, or anywhere else on the church property. I stood there, amazed, and described to my friend the dream I had had a few years earlier in Southeast Asia. I was sure it was a sign from God that my father's death was just around the corner. Two weeks later, my father was gone. I asked my pastor if he knew where the picnic table had come from and he said, "No one knows where it came from."

I believe this was a gift from God to prepare me for what was about to happen. I am grateful and humbled that the Lord rescued my father and has reserved a place for him in Heaven.

MY PATH INTO THE
WORLD OF SECRETS

As I've stated in earlier chapters, my addiction began with my very first exposure to my father's stash of pornography as a nine-year-old boy. My body and mind were not mature enough or developed enough to understand what I was looking at.

The *stash* today is taking on new forms. In my generation, the stash was a stack of black and white men's magazines, showing topless women with a great deal left to the imagination. As time has progressed, today's stash can be a number of things that are very different. The stash can be a hard drive on a computer where files are hidden deeply on the computer system's file structure. The stash can be a portable drive that can be hidden from site and accessed during any moment of privacy. The stash can also be pictures or movies stored on a handheld device like a cell phone. The stash can also be sexually explicit images embedded in cell phone text messages. One thing is for sure, the images in a person's stash are much more explicit and detailed than ever before.

As a child of an alcoholic, I was already at risk of becoming an alcoholic. In the early years of my experimentation, I only had access to pornographic materials sporadically. Weeks could go by before I could safely sneak a peek at my dad's growing magazine collection. As I grew older, I discovered masturbation and quickly reinforced my habit by pleasing myself as often as I could without being discovered.

As I became a teenager, I gained a little more access to pornography through classmates and friends. It wasn't unusual to have a classmate show up at junior high school with a shoplifted or hijacked *Playboy* or *Penthouse* magazine. The boys treated these like gold, with only privileged friends getting a turn to feast their eyes on the latest centerfold.

I remember trying to act cool with the other guys, treating each new viewing session as something that wasn't that out of the ordinary, while secretly wishing I could take the magazine home and spend hours lusting and fantasizing about the women.

During my high school years, the magazines took a definite turn toward more enticing and explicit images. Instead of just showing topless women, they began to show full-frontal nudity. Movies at the theaters began showing more nudity and even occasionally included simulated sex acts. I remember when *Hustler* magazine started hitting the shelves in stores. The public was outraged, yet I'm sure their sales went through the roof. I couldn't get enough. Yet, the more explicit the images, the more it took to get the same rush. I still didn't know it yet, but this was the first sign that my addiction had taken root deep into my soul. In a lot of ways, I was no different from the drug addict that kept requiring more and more of the drug to get high. At the time, I didn't make the connection. I just knew I needed to find the next hidden or taboo sexual escapade to feed my appetite.

In high school, I met my future wife. As our relationship grew, I felt a great sense of connection to her that was totally different from all of my porn mistresses. This was real. This was someone with whom I could have a conversation. This was someone with whom I could build a life and a future. I desired her for so much more than sex. It was a strange feeling. Up to this point, I thought I could be happy with a smorgasbord of magazines and movies. I realized there was so much more to a real relationship, and I wanted to experience it all with someone I truly loved and someone who truly loved me.

At the age of seventeen, my wife and I were married. We were young, inexperienced, and probably, in hindsight, stupid for getting married so early. We didn't have a clue. For the first year or so, we enjoyed that honeymoon period that so many couples experience. We experienced joy, happiness, contentment, and a bonding together that was genuine, yet not quite fully developed. Then the joy and happiness began to turn to disagreements, disappointments, arguments, and questioning. Like so many other young couples, the typical sources of couples' disagreement entered our marriage. With my history of pornography use and family abuse, the difficulties caused me to avoid conflict instead of discussing my feelings and emotions. I would basically shut down. My way of dealing with my emotions was to seek out that which relieved my stress.

The solution seems so simple now, looking back. I should have opened up to my wife and shared my feelings and emotions with her when I was disappointed, hurt, or angry. Instead, I became quiet and unattached. Instead of seeking her out and asking for her forgiveness when I was wrong, I stuffed my feelings and let anger and resentment build within me. My wife felt the distance and instinctively knew something was wrong, but I would lie or make excuses about my alienation.

My secret porn use was causing major relationship problems in my marriage. The more I resisted opening up, the more deeply I delved into more explicit pornography. This was my outlet or my way of numbing my feelings. I had started the same pattern that was present in my alcoholic father. At an early age, I remember making a pledge to God that I would never become an alcoholic like my father. I had kept that pledge, but I instead chose a different beverage—the beverage of sexual fantasy and lust. And I drank my fill.

Things have drastically changed since I first viewed my father's stash in 1965. The Internet has changed everything! Every person who has Internet access is now at risk. If you have children, you need to wake up to the danger of the computer screen in their room. If they are not addicted today, they can be addicted tomorrow.

My path into the world of secrets started at home. I didn't receive any help from my parents, because there was an unwritten rule that we didn't talk about sexual things. My parents had their own issues that prevented them from healthy parenting.

I became a Christian at the age of thirteen. Surely the Church could help me. Would church be the place where I could learn about healthy human sexuality? Would church finally be the place where I would learn how to overcome this secret behavior? What would my church teach me about sex? It turns out that the churches I was a part of also treated sex as something they didn't talk about. Once again, I was left to find my way out of the terrible pit on my own.

As I began to search for the answers about what God thought about sex, I examined the Bible for clues, instructions, and clear teaching. It becomes obvious after one searches through the scriptures that there is a lot we have to figure out on our own. The lack of teaching by the Church about sex shows that the Church and sex go together like vinegar and water. I'll share what I've learned about God and sex in the next chapter.

GOD & SEX

If you are a typical male, you probably looked at the table of contents and jumped to this chapter first. If you are an average male with an average level of testosterone, anything with "SEX" in the title will get your attention. If you did, go ahead and read this chapter, then start over at the beginning. You're quite normal!

God designed sex. He made it to be something enjoyable and pleasurable between a man and woman joined together in a holy matrimony.

So, why is it so hard for us to talk about sex? Why do pastors avoid the topic like the H1N1 flu bug? Why do churches offer help only after men and women get into trouble? Why are churches failing to teach about healthy human sexuality?

One word: *fear*! What percentage of today's adults do you think have had the *sex talk*? What percentage of today's adults had a clue about sex after the *sex talk* with one or both of their parents? Most of the men and women I meet didn't have a *sex talk* at all. Why are parents so afraid to talk about sex with their children?

Most parents aren't comfortable talking about sex, because their parent's weren't comfortable talking about sex. Many parents inherited their parent's belief that sex is not to be talked about. Sex is an embarrassing, uncomfortable topic for most parents. They think, "What if little Johnnie asks me a tough question?"

Here's one theory (it's my theory, so take it for what it's worth). Our society has moved away from an agriculturally based economy to a city-based economy. The vast majority of people do not live on farms anymore. In past generations, nearly everyone was raised on a farm or worked on a farm. I hate to get graphic here, but when you grow up on a farm there are a lot of animals procreating all of the time. Little eyes growing up around animals figure out what sex is pretty fast. It was not uncommon for the family to talk around the dinner table about bringing in a bull to fertilize a heifer or multiply the herd. It wasn't perverted; it was natural and part of the process of life. Life continued because of sex. Babies or little calves were born because of what the boy bull did with the girl cow. Animals provided an easy way for children to naturally learn about reproduction. Children's natural curiosity led them to ask questions. Parents could answer their questions using the examples the children saw during a normal day.

Fast forward to today's world—parents avoid the *sex talk* entirely. It's not uncommon to hear a father say, "He'll learn on the street just like I did." If you don't teach your children, then who will? What examples do our children see to learn about sex? Stew on that answer for a little while. *Reality* television teaches that sex is fun, acceptable, risk free, safe, and requires that everyone feel good all of the time. What is shown today in movies, television, and pornography rarely teaches about the natural tensions in real relationships that are an integral part of healthy human sexuality.

Church is probably the worst place to learn about human sexuality, because the church is almost completely silent on the topic. The Bible is not silent about sex, but its instructions about sex are pretty general. There is a lot that God wanted the husband and wife to figure out on their own.

God designed marriage. The first marriage occurred when God created Adam and provided a helpmate for him, Eve. This union, or marriage, was approved, designed, and ordained by God. This was our first example of marriage. Together, Adam and Eve sinned and were separated from God. However, they were not separated from each other. God's plan to multiply the earth with offspring began with Adam and Eve in the Garden of Eden.

> God blessed them and said to them, be fruitful and increase in number; fill the earth and subdue it. Rule over the fish in the sea and the birds in the sky and over every living creature that moves on the ground.
>
> Genesis 1:28 (NIV)

As far as we know, God didn't leave an instruction manual behind. Adam and Eve had to figure out this "be fruitful and multiply" thing.

Commitment in marriage is a result of making a holy covenant with God; each marriage partner vows before God to remain faithful to his or her partner. Women are to submit to their husbands.

> For this is the way the holy women of the past who put their hope in God used to adorn themselves. They submitted themselves to their own husbands.
>
> 1 Peter, 3:5 (NIV)

Husbands are to treat their wives with respect so that their prayers will not be hindered:

> Husbands, in the same way be considerate as you live with your wives, and treat them with respect as the weaker partner and as heirs with you of the gracious gift of life, so that nothing will hinder your prayers.
>
> 1 Peter 3:7 (NIV)

The scriptures are clear that sexual infidelity is wrong. Jesus even said that any form of thought related to unfaithfulness is a sin.

> But I tell you that anyone who looks at a woman lustfully has already committed adultery with her in his heart."
>
> Matthew 5:28 (NIV)

The Bible is relatively silent about what are acceptable practices in the area of sexual relations between a husband and wife. However, Paul writes to the church in Corinth:

> Now for the matters you wrote about: It is good for a man not to have sexual relations with a woman. But since sexual immorality is occurring, each man should have sexual relations with his own wife, and each woman with her own husband. The husband should fulfill his marital duty to his wife, and likewise the wife to her husband. The wife does not have authority over her own body but yields it to her husband. In the same way, the husband does not have authority over his own body but yields it to his wife. Do not deprive each other except perhaps by mutual consent and for a time, so that you may devote yourselves to prayer. Then come together again so that Satan will not tempt you because of your lack of self-control.

> 1 Corinthians 7:1-5 (NIV)

Self-control was a problem in Paul's time too. Not too different from today, is it?

The husband and wife are to fulfill their sexual, marital duties to each other. The attitude each should take is that they do not have authority over their own bodies. Depriving a wife or husband, except for a time of prayer, is not wise. Self-control will become an issue at some point. Sexual intimacy is left to the husband and the wife's discretion. The specifics of sexual intimacy in a marriage should honor each person, be edifying to God, and show respect for the other partner's comfort.

I'm not a Bible scholar, but it seems clear to me that God intentionally challenged the man and woman who were united in marriage to discover what is acceptable and pleasing to God and each other. That can be very different from couple-to-couple. This idea requires and shouts out to us that constant, open communication must happen in a marriage all of the time. There are no exceptions, no hesitation, and no reading the latest *seven steps to a fulfilling sexual relationship* book with your spouse. The best guide is sitting down, or lying down in this case, and figuring it all out. After all, isn't that the best part of discovering your mate's wants and desires? Practice, practice, practice!

Okay, after that last paragraph, if you are ready to tie me to a cross and crucify me for blasphemy, you might be one of the people in church who hold back others in understanding and enjoying the gift of sex that God has provided. Again, it was designed to be enjoyed in a spirit-filled marital union between a man and a woman.

Sex is a beautiful, God-designed experience that creates a unique bond between two committed, married adults. Marriage without healthy, mutually satisfying sex is not marriage, it is cohabitation. Marriage without faithfulness is not marriage; it is a field of land mines waiting to be detonated. Marriage without healthy, mutually satisfying sex is a marriage without intimacy, trust, and satisfaction and is headed for trouble.

In the next chapter, we will look at the research on the Internet and addiction and how the risks have increased with its use. Don't think your family will be the only one who resists temptation. Don't simply believe that you are strong enough to resist temptation on your own. The research shows that anyone is vulnerable. Christians are especially at risk!

THE TRUTH ABOUT
THE INTERNET &
ADDICTION

This may be the most boring chapter in *My Father's Stash*, yet it may also be the most important. Everyone reading this book should be well-educated on how much of an impact the Internet has had on dangerous, addictive behavior. The findings may surprise you. If you are already trapped, you won't be surprised.

I want you to understand that this is not my opinion. This information comes from reliable sources and is fully credited in the reference section. Please don't skip this chapter! You, your children, and the generations of your family that will come after you need to know what is happening and how dangerous the Internet can be.

According to Internet researcher P. Saari, Internet use has been an issue for men since the invention and propagation of this electronic medium. Christian men have also struggled with the Internet and its many uses. As the Internet has become more accessible to private individuals, issues of addiction, in the form of time using this technology, has begun to increase. Saari further notes that, "The technology caught on, and by spring 1998, it was estimated that the Internet, which was made more accessible by the innovation of the World Wide Web, was being used by more than 50,000,000 people."[1]

The Internet is now readily available on a variety of personal and business technology equipment; therefore, individuals no longer have to travel or search to gain access to addictive behaviors, but rather can access the Internet from their own home, their office, or their cell phone. Internet use has been encouraged at churches of many denominations to communicate with their members and provide information about their churches. Additionally, it is often a form of communicating information related to Christian conferences and audience interaction (i.e., live surveys, online statistics sharing, and online presentations).

The Internet was invented in the late 1960s by the US Department of Defense.[2] By 2011, the Internet had become a part of everyday living around the world. In 2002, 59 percent of Americans responded that they used the Internet at least occasionally. In 2008, 74 percent of Americans responded that they had used the Internet at least occasionally. This is a dramatic increase from 2002 to 2008.[2] Men and women used the Internet almost equally overly this time: men 48.1 percent and women 51.9 percent[3] (Internet Access and Usage in the U.S., Fall, 2007). In fact, Internet use has become so pervasive that over 58 percent indicated they used this form of media over consulting the experts like doctors, lawyers, or financial gurus.[4] By 2007, it was found that 77 percent of Americans had regular Internet access. A large percentage, 64 percent, had a broadband connection, while only 13 percent had slower dial-up access.[4] This ultimately indicates that the Internet is readily available to a large percentage of the American population and is continuing to grow. By 2011, a whole generation had never lived without access to the Internet, and Americans frequent Internet use has grown to 79 percent.[5]

Internet Access

Access to the Internet is no longer limited to the use of a hard-wired desktop computer. In response to a survey by the Pew Report, 62 percent of Americans had accessed the Internet using a wireless device or used nonvoice data applications. On any given day, 42 percent of Americans had used their cell phone or other wireless device to access a nonvoice data application. These data applications include texting, emailing, and taking or sending a picture or video.[6]

Addiction Defined

Addiction is defined as a "compulsive need for and use of a habit-forming substance (as heroin, nicotine, or alcohol) characterized by tolerance and by well-defined physiological symptoms upon withdrawal; broadly: persistent compulsive use of a substance known by the user to be harmful."

There have been attempts to include a variety of behavioral addictions into the general category of substance addictions. Many other behavioral addictions, such as Internet addiction, gambling, sex addiction, pornography addiction, and others have not been classified by the Diagnostic and Statistical Manual of Mental Disorders (DSM) as clinical addictions. Several of the behavioral addictions have shown similarities to substance addictions.[7] There is some controversy within the research community about which non-substance addictions to include as addictions. Further research has been suggested.

There are commonalities between substance addiction and behavioral addictions. Compulsive behavior is characteristic in both substance and behavioral addictions. Related to all addictions is increased compulsivity. Negative behaviors continue, even though the individual understands the negative consequences. Addiction has been found to be genetically linked. A person's environment plays a role in addiction; however, there can be familial roles as well. An individual with one addiction usually has other addictions present. The alcoholic may also be addicted to drugs. The drug addict may also be addicted to gambling. Treatment consists of "four main psychotherapies: cognitive-behavioral therapy (CBT), 12-Step facilitation therapy (TSF), motivational enhancement therapy (MET), and social and behavioral network therapy (SBNT)."[8] Therapists have begun to apply traditional addiction therapy to other behavioral addictions. Traditional therapy treatments have shown effective results in treating other behavioral addictions. The best reported results are those that individualize the treatment for each individual.[8]

Internet Addiction

Researcher Aviv Weinstein, in an addiction study in 2010, showed that as the Internet has grown in use, Internet addiction has become more prevalent. It is estimated that up to 8.2 percent of the general population has an addiction to Internet use. Internet addiction has also been correlated to psychiatric disorders, depression, anxiety disorders, and attention deficit hyperactivity disorder (ADHD).[9] While there is no recognition of Internet addiction in the Diagnostic and Statistical Manual of Mental Disorder (DSM), counselors and mental health officials are seeing an increase in the number of reported cases of Internet addiction and its associated behavioral problems.

Weinstein and Lejoyeux claim that, "Problematic Internet use, or addiction, is characterized by excessive or poorly controlled preoccupations, urges, or behaviors regarding Internet use that leads to impairment or distress."[9] Problematic Internet use is also generally defined as individuals who have problems with online pornography and gambling. In a broader range, problematic Internet use can include online behaviors that affect relationships, personal values, obligations, and the well-being of a person's mental or physical state.[10] A survey of mental health providers by Mitchell (2009) identified eleven types of problematic behaviors associated with Internet use.

1. Overuse of the Internet
2. Internet pornography use
3. Sexual exploitation and abuse
4. Online infidelity
5. Gaming, gambling, or fantasy role-play
6. Harassment
7. Isolative-avoidant behavior
8. Fraud, stealing, or deception
9. Failed online relationships
10. Harmful material
11. Risky or inappropriate use not otherwise specified[10]

The mental health clinicians labeled the eleven behaviors problematic, because the behaviors negatively impacted the clients' "lives in the areas of family and intimate relationship (e.g., divorce, parent-child conflict) work (e.g., loss of job) school (e.g. failing grades, disciplinary problems) the law (e.g., arrest) victimization, aggression, and mental health (e.g., depression, anxiety) issues."[10]

Five of the top eleven problematic behaviors identified by mental health providers are related to risky behavior associated with Internet use: (1) overuse of the Internet, (2) the use of Internet pornography, sexual exploitation, and online infidelity, (3) harassment, (4) fraud, stealing, etc. and (5) gambling.

These problems may become particularly problematic if the individual considers himself/herself to be a Christian and tries to hide the addiction.

Research indicates and confirms that there are many problematic behaviors that can be associated with frequent Internet use. Christian men were included as a subgroup in the research general findings.

Internet Pornography

Research indicated Internet pornography provided a significant, additional addiction risk for men. Forty-seven percent of Christian men said pornography was a major problem in the home. Internet pornography is a 13 billion dollar industry and comprised approximately 12 percent of all Internet traffic. In America, it is estimated that 13 percent of the Internet traffic is associated with pornography and 75 percent of the viewers are male. The United States produces 89 percent of the world's Internet pornography web pages.[11] As the Internet has become more available, the proliferation of adult Web sites has also grown exponentially. There were 14 million identified pages of pornography in 1998. By August 2005, there were more than 15 billion pages of adult content. That indicates a 107,042 percent increase. With this increase in the number of adult sites, the different ways to access the Internet has also grown. With the improvement in the speed of technology, more images, videos, and downloads are available. Images are more intense and detailed than ever before. In a survey of 84 college-age males at a rural, western university, it was found that 20-60 percent of the sample that had viewed Internet pornography found that it was problematic. Of the respondents, 87 percent of the males and 31 percent of the females indicated that they agreed that viewing Internet pornography was acceptable. Portions of the males (20 percent in the Twohig study) who viewed Internet pornography believed it was unacceptable. The Twohig (2009) study found that 17 percent of the individuals in the study met criteria, which indicated that their viewing of Internet pornography was problematic even though a large majority said it was acceptable.[13]

The same associations for general Internet addiction were indicated for Internet pornography addiction. Behaviors of being compulsive, impulsive, and difficulty in controlling behavior were present in Internet pornography addiction. For those individuals who viewed Internet pornography on a regular basis, there was an increased reporting of "depression, social isolation, damaged relationships, career loss, or decreased productivity, and financial consequences as a result of their behaviors."[13]

The Twohig (2009) study summarized that viewing Internet pornography was problematic for some, but it was not problematic for everyone. However, 58.54 percent of the respondents who viewed Internet pornography reported that they had experienced negative behavioral outcomes. This indicates that there is a great risk for anyone who may view Internet pornography. There is also a direct correlation between the viewing of Internet pornography and fears about legal consequences, loss of productivity, spiritual/religious conflicts, shame, guilt, and the impact on relationships.

One surprising result of the Twohig study was the indication that the greater the individual tries to control the viewing of Internet pornography, the more the individual will struggle with controlling the viewing.[13] This finding would validate the need for more in-depth research to determine the relationship between Internet pornography and conventional addiction therapies.

Religiosity and Internet Pornography Viewing

Previous studies have shown that religiosity has been a protective factor in problem behaviors such as delinquency, crime, alcoholism, and substance abuse.[14] There have been few studies to determine if there is also a protective factor for Internet pornography use among Christians. The Baltazar (2010) study surveyed 751 males and females at a Christian university in the Midwest. The vast majority of respondents, 97.4 percent, identified themselves as having the same religious affiliation as the Church of the university.[15] Intentional viewing of Internet pornography varied greatly between men and women—68 percent and 22 percent, respectively. The number of males who reported viewing Internet pornography in the last week was also significantly different than females—males 22 percent and females 2 percent. The top three reported negative consequences for viewing Internet pornography for Christian males were:

1. Worsened relationship with God/Christ;
2. Led to an increase in their sexual behavior;
3. Increased negative emotions (e.g., guilt, shame, low self-esteem, etc.)[15]

One significant factor in the Baltazar (2010) study was that the male's heavy Internet pornography use (six hours or more per week) was 50 percent below other studies in the frequency of viewing Internet pornography while on campus. It must be noted that this Midwest university used Internet filtering to deter and prevent Internet pornography viewing by individuals using university resources. While there are ways around almost all Internet filters, this was a significant deterrent for the students in the survey. Sixty-seven percent of Internet pornography viewing in the study occurred at home.

There is also a link between Internet pornography use and frequency of alcohol and drug use and the number of sex partners. Combining these behaviors added to the susceptibility to risky Internet behavior.[15]

The Baltazar (2010) study advised universities to address the risks and dangers associated with Internet pornography use among their students. Christian men, and to a lesser extent Christian women, who viewed Internet pornography may have to deal with significant spiritual and behavioral consequences. Since most Internet pornography viewing was done at home in the Baltazar (2010) study, and the results were so dramatically impacted, it is critical that churches and parents use Internet filtering software to deter or prevent unwanted exposure to Internet pornography.

Christian Men, Internet Pornography, and the Impact on Marriage

Marriages are impacted negatively by the use of Internet pornography by Christian men. Christian couples are especially vulnerable to the damages caused by Internet pornography viewing. Healthy sexuality has been a taboo topic in church culture. Deviant sexuality has been an even more taboo topic in church culture. Church denominational leaders rarely address Internet pornography use, which leads to the conclusion that healthy sexuality has not been addressed in church culture.[16]

Due to the lack of teaching in the church about healthy sexuality, the perception by Christian males is that any addiction relating to human sexuality will be met with little or no compassion or understanding. The perception that there will be negative responses to admitting a personal struggle with a possible addiction has prevented Christian men and couples from seeking effective treatment for addictive, problematic behaviors.

Internet pornography use is incompatible with a stable, happy, and healthy marriage. The inability to sexually relate to a marriage partner leads to a negative attitude about sexual intimacy. An inflated importance of sexual relations develops. A separation of emotional involvement between partners will also be prevalent. Internet pornography distorts reality as it relates to a healthy marriage and sexuality.[17]

Internet pornography provides Christian men with a fantasy world of sexual success with no portrayed negative consequences. The fallacy of the Internet world is that the viewed online relationships never have problems. Problems, disagreements, and challenges that occur in every marriage do not occur in this fantasy world. Men isolate themselves from marriage relationship problems and do not face conflict.[16]

Clergy are especially vulnerable to problematic Internet behaviors. The factors influencing clergy involve inadequate sexuality development, isolation, and consequences.[16] Clergy face multiple layers of consequences if they are discovered. This manifests itself with increased isolation, fear of discovery, and fear of losing their jobs. Reaching a point of seeking help for problematic behaviors is especially difficult for clergy.

Christian men consider sexual addiction to be different from all other addictions. Christian men perceive sexual addictions as moral failures. Christian men believe sexual addiction is treated differently in church culture. Because of this perception, Christian men are much more reluctant to seek help and share their struggle with another person, their clergy, or a counselor.[16]

The consequences of isolation, weak emotional bonding to their partner, objectification of their female partners, and the increased likelihood of extramarital affairs places Christian marriages at high risk of failure.[16]

My wife and I recently received a phone call and were asked to speak to a woman who is divorcing her husband. She has asked her husband to leave, because their marriage has fallen apart. Her husband has repeatedly tried to get his wife to participate in watching pornography with him. This had left her feeling unloved and unworthy as a wife and woman. She felt that this behavior is degrading to her and the women who were in the pornography. She could not understand why the man who said, "I do," cannot say, "I won't," when it came to pornography. She was torn apart inside, because she felt she could not satisfy her husband sexually or emotionally. She felt dirty and rejected. Her husband told her that she was a "prude." "All men do it" was his constant message. He believed that viewing porn together would strengthen their lovemaking and improve their intimacy. He was going to *do it* no matter what, so she should join him to satisfy *her man*.

My heart breaks, hearing this story. Unfortunately, this situation happens all too often. How could a man believe that bringing other women (or men) into their sexual relationship could *improve* their relationship? What has happened to the belief of marriage being one man and one woman living faithfully with each other for life? How can people be so influenced by society and their own perversions that they drag other people down with them?

The belief that watching images or a movie of others is going to do anything to help a relationship is an absolute lie. Something happens to a person's value and belief system when they believe that being intimate with someone else—while being in a committed relationship—is *normal* or *good*.

Sexually healthy men want real intimacy in their relationship, whether that is with a spouse, fiancé, or girlfriend. For a guy, real intimacy is all about the feeling of total acceptance, love, and respect. While sex is important in a relationship, the distorted view of sex being the most important part of a relationship will not lead to true intimacy. True intimacy includes great sex in a committed relationship where both partners feel safe, accepted, and loved. Every relationship has problems. Finding ways to deal with the challenges is part of growing more intimate over time.

What do you believe about sex and intimacy in your relationship? Have you allowed images of other people to be placed ahead of your lifelong partner? This will certainly have consequences as you navigate through life. If you can replace those explicit images of women—other than your spouse—with thoughts and images of your committed partner, you can go a long way toward building a more intimate, fulfilling, and rewarding relationship.

Don't allow your value and belief system to be *swayed* by the garbage that is thrown your way. You must always be on guard. You must also guard your spouse and children. The pornography industry has a plan to capture you and your family. Do you have a plan to protect them?

WHAT THE RESEARCH TELLS US

The research review indicates that Internet use has escalated dramatically since its invention, development, and propagation. With this escalation and increased availability, the potential for risky behaviors has also increased. Internet addiction has increased. Negative consequences associated with addictive patterns have increased. Christian men, as a subgroup of the general population, have the same level of access to the Internet. Technology development has also increased the availability and convenience of accessing online material and data, anywhere, at any time. The Internet has become a trusted source for information, news, commentary, and preliminary research.

Internet addiction has been a growing phenomenon. Significant research needs to be done to understand and diagnose the causes of Internet addiction. Effective treatments need to be identified and developed. Internet addiction has been related to other psychiatric disorders. Counselors are reporting increased cases of

Internet addiction. Mental health officials have been reporting a significant increase in negative outcomes for individuals and families.

Christian men are susceptible to and actively involved in viewing Internet pornography. Viewing Internet pornography is problematic for men. Not all men are at risk of addiction by viewing Internet pornography, though. For Christian men, there is a greater risk due to their religiosity. Feelings of shame, guilt, and isolation increase their risk in not being able to overcome problematic behaviors without professional counseling or spiritual guidance.

The failure of churches to teach about healthy sexuality creates an impression among Christian men that sexual sin is not acceptable. Christian men often believe that other addictions (i.e. alcoholism, drug dependency, etc.) are more acceptable to the Church. This view, whether it is accurate or not, adds to the isolation and causes Christian men to avoid counseling or spiritual advice for their problematic behaviors. Trying to control the viewing of Internet pornography can actually lessen the person's effectiveness in stopping the viewing.

Viewing Internet pornography damages relationships and marriages. A majority of men who view Internet pornography report that they have experienced negative behavioral outcomes. Viewing Internet pornography could lead to confused views about sexuality, intimacy, and marriage partner relationships. The importance of sexual relationships becomes distorted, and expectations of healthy sexuality are confused. The picture that is painted in the Internet pornography world is one of sexual intimacy without any problems or conflict. This distorts Christian men's views about expectations in marriage, causing men to isolate themselves and live in an online fantasy world. Marriage partners also become isolated and less emotionally attached due to neglect or lack of communication and intimacy. Internet pornography increases the likelihood of marital infidelity, separation, and divorce.[16]

The most significant risk identified in the literature review for Christian men is Internet pornography. The problematic outcome of viewing Internet pornography impacts individuals and families and is a growing problem. The research indicates that more should be done to provide information, teaching, counseling, remedies, and solutions for this growing problem.

If you made it through the research findings you're probably ready to move on to something else more interesting. Let me share a story that demonstrates how much is at stake for individuals and families and how the Internet has changed the game.

One man, we'll call him Bill (name changed to protect his identity), shared with a men's accountability group how he had struggled all of his life with pornography. Bill was raised in a good family with Christian parents. He didn't have a history of addiction in his family. He grew up attending church and became a Christian at a young age. Bill's first exposure to pornography was around the age of thirteen. Pornography wasn't really a problem for him until he went to college. At college, the lure of pornography once again returned. Bill met his future wife in college and soon was married. Again, the monster of pornography took a backseat... for a little while. Bill shared that he had long periods of not using pornography and really didn't see it as a big problem in his life. Then the Internet came on the scene. This changed everything. Instead of having the deterrent of someone seeing him purchase a magazine, Bill could now access an unending parade of beauties on his computer screen in complete isolation. For him, this is when the beast began to gain control of his life. Bill would have some extended periods of not looking at the pixilated, provocative images. Yet, they always seemed to draw him back.

As a Christian man, he felt completely alone in his struggle. A few years ago, Bill joined a men's group where men share their most significant challenges. These are small groups of men, six to twelve in number, who pledge together to keep what is said in the group confidential. They must each sign a confidentiality agreement. A curriculum of Bible-study material is offered, but the primary goal is to create strong, bonded relationships between the men.

During the very first meeting, the moderator of the group began sharing his personal story. Bill recounted how his heart began pounding in his throat. The moderator shared a similar story to Bill's own. The moderator finished and asked the men in the circle if anyone else was willing to share his story and describe what his biggest struggle is as a Christian man. Bill watched and listened in amazement as, one by one, each man began to open up and share his struggles for the first time. That day, men shared their stories of addiction to pornography, gambling, alcohol, and even past molestations. One man was struggling with making a decision to leave his wife.

A lingering moment of silence filled the room. Would Bill open up and finally tell his story to the men in this group? Bill was wondering if the men would crucify him. Could he really trust these guys? After all, he and his family had been attending this church for years. They were actively involved in ministry in a lot of different areas. Would this be the end of his ministry, or would this be the day he let these men see who he really was?

Gathering his courage, Bill began sharing his lifelong struggle with pornography. When he finished he felt as if a million-pound weight had been lifted off of his shoulders. The freedom Bill felt was energizing and uplifting. The men in the group each felt the same relief. Many of the men wept as they shared. They had finally found a safe place to share their secret struggles.

The best part of this story is that the men in that circle listened intently to some really difficult things and still found a place in their heart to love and accept each other. Instantly, the men had bonded together. Their relationships instantly became strong and enduring. They experienced love and forgiveness from each other.

It was a beautiful thing to witness, and it happens all of the time in these men's groups.

Getting men to attend a group like this is a challenge. If they know what is going to happen ahead of time, they will avoid the groups like the Bubonic plague. We start these groups slowly and prayerfully with a Bible-based curriculum. As relationships and comfort begins to take hold, we then have the moderator share his story. While every moderator's story is different, there are always many common themes that surface in the group (Note that the moderator doesn't always share his story the first time the group meets, like Bill's moderator did). We build on the commonalities of the struggles to help and support the men in the groups.

Unlike most Bible studies I've been a part of, we don't have trouble getting guys to stay in the groups. As a matter of fact, we often struggle to get them to take a week off. Ever had that problem with a traditional Bible study?

Just a few months later, as Bill was weighing whether to confess his struggle with pornography use to his wife, Bill's young daughter came to him and his wife and admitted that she had been looking at pornography on a handheld, web-enabled device. It had never crossed Bill's mind that his daughter could access porn on this portable device.

His daughter explained to them that she had been doing homework on their family computer when a pop-up came up that piqued her curiosity. She clicked on the link and it took her to a pornographic Web site. She immediately closed the window, but was later drawn back to the Web site, curious, nervous, and motivated to find more. Bill's daughter then told her mom and dad that she had progressed to full-blown, deviant, BDSM Web sites. She was frightened and scared, saying that she felt "out-of-control." She felt embarrassed and humiliated that she had gone to these Web sites and begged her parents for forgiveness.

Bill was heartbroken that his daughter had experienced such shame and guilt. Bill was also disgusted with himself that he hadn't protected his own daughter from the very thing that he had been struggling with his whole life. Since his wife still didn't know his own struggle, he felt more shame and guilt that he had not disclosed to his wife the truth about himself. Bill's daughter had not taken years to become addicted. She became a full-blown addict in three months!

What has changed in today's culture is that there is now a common, easily accessible stream of temptations that can be viewed in complete privacy without the fear of discovery. The Internet has put everyone at risk of falling into the trap of addiction. The pornography industry knows how to suck you in.

From Jerry Ropelato, Chief Technology Officer for ContentWatch, Inc., makers of Net Nanny:

> There was a time when tricking a teen into viewing pornography meant that his pals

pasted a *Playboy* centerfold into his locker. On the other hand, if he went looking for it, he could've gotten hold of a magazine or two through an unscrupulous store clerk or a friend's older brother. But once those few pages had exhausted their appeal, there was no full-scale blitz to deluge him with more.

Times have changed. Not only is pornography today more lewd and provocative, but its peddlers (now part of a multi-billion dollar industry) are much more aggressive in their recruitment of new customers. For both sides, the Internet has offered up a crucial ingredient to the burgeoning industry-anonymity. No need to leave one's home to purchase pornography. Now, a never-ending supply of ever more erotic and interactive pornography can be accessed and experienced in a completely private world. And now, teen boys aren't the sole targets. To a pornographer, anyone with a computer is a potential addict.

Just about anyone who has used the Internet-from 7-year-old boys to 80-year-old grandmothers-knows that pornography is just a click away. But most Internet users still believe that unless they go looking for porn, it won't find them. What they don't realize, however, is how aggressively pornographers are implementing new strategies in marketing and technology to actually push pornography to unwitting users, without their consent, and often even without their knowledge.[23]

Here is a list of the methods, tools, and loopholes pornographers use to lure you:

> Deception, Porn-Napping, Cyber Squatting, Doorway Scams, Misspelling, Advertising, Entrapment, Looping, Mousetrapping, Startup File Alteration, Cookies, Dangerous Downloads, Trojan Horses, Dialers, Spyware, Live Action, Email, Mail Spoofing, Chat, File Sharing, Peer-To-Peer, and Bulletin Boards
> To understand what each of these is, visit: *http://www.strengthenthefamily.net/tricks_ pornographers.php*

Protecting yourself and your family has never been a greater challenge.

While the research gives us many clues on how to prevent addictive behavior, I always wanted Jesus to simply take away my addictive behavior. If I could pray to Jesus, the Son of God, why wouldn't He answer my prayer and remove all of my sexual urges and unhealthy behaviors?

IS JESUS ENOUGH?

I have to admit, there were times I didn't think that Jesus was enough. When I was in the deepest pit of my addiction, I often asked God why He wouldn't answer my prayer to take away my addiction. As I've said, it seemed as if God was silent, had His face turned away, or was simply too busy with someone else to provide a *quick-fix* for my addiction. Looking back now, I was really looking for an easy way out. Finding out the truth about addiction and realizing how hard it was going to be to reset my mind and change my patterns of behavior, I would have been doomed to fall back into my addiction if God had just conveniently zapped me with a bolt of lightning.

Is Jesus enough? Yes, He absolutely is! In my case, Jesus didn't rattle me with an earthquake, shake my soul, and rid me of my desires and lusts. Instead, Jesus was and is an always-present helper, comforter, and friend. I believe Jesus wanted me to do the hard work. Jesus wanted me to experience my shame and guilt so that I would remember the hurt and pain I caused others. Could Jesus have removed all of my lustful desires for the rest of my life? Absolutely! Jesus, however, didn't cleanse me on day one. He didn't cleanse me on day two or day three. As a matter of fact, Jesus didn't cleanse me in month one, two, or three. Jesus did forgive me instantly, each time I asked for forgiveness. However, Jesus wanted me to get to a place of strength so that I could defeat the many temptations that would come my way. It's one thing to constantly ask for forgiveness; it's another thing to be in a healthy, spiritual place that allows me to defeat my enemy, Satan. Will Jesus forgive me every time I fail? Yes, yes, yes! But Jesus will allow me to experience the consequences of my sin to learn how to defeat it in the future.

"Godly sorrow brings repentance that leads to salvation and leaves no regret, but worldly sorrow brings death" (2 Corinthians, 7:10, NIV).

My sorrow needs to be so deep and intense that it is an admission to God that I have sinned against Him and Him alone. If I experience this kind of Godly sorrow, then I am expressing true repentance. Once I reach this point of repentance, then I will be led to a wonderful place that has no regrets. No regrets? At first I thought I would never be able to reach a place of no regrets. I still struggle with thoughts of what I did in my addiction and how it hurt so many people that I love. However, the longer I have been in recovery, I have begun to see how God has chosen to use my past to help others. How can I regret something that God is using in such a powerful way?

If I had tried to express my sorrow simply through my own efforts, I know I wouldn't have done the hard work that is required for recovery. I would have tried to fix everything myself. This never worked for me. It won't work for you either. I have met hundreds of men who have been caught by their wives either using pornography, texting inappropriate messages, or have been caught in full-blown affairs. It is rare for these men to truly repent and express true, Godly sorrow. Most of the time, they are sorry they got caught. They straighten up for a while and then fall back into their old patterns.

While forgiveness is available for anyone who asks, Jesus doesn't promise that you will be *sin-free* going forward. In other words, Jesus forgives, but you have to change your life so that you won't fall into sin anymore. Look at the often-quoted bible story of the woman caught in adultery in the book of John, chapter eight:

> The teachers of the law and the Pharisees brought in a woman caught in adultery. They made her stand before the group and said to Jesus, "Teacher, this woman was caught in the act of adultery. In the Law, Moses commanded us to stone such women. Now what do you say?" They were using this question as a trap, in order to have a basis for accusing him.
>
> But Jesus bent down and started to write on the ground with his finger. When they kept on questioning him, he straightened up and said to them, "Let any one of you who is without sin be the first to throw a stone at her." Again he stooped down and wrote on the ground.

> At this, those who heard began to go away one at a time, the older ones first, until only Jesus was left, with the woman still standing there. Jesus straightened up and asked her,
>
> "Woman, where are they? Has no one condemned you?"
>
> "No one, sir," she said.
>
> "Then neither do I condemn you," Jesus declared. "Go now and leave your life of sin."
>
> John 8:3-11 (NIV)

Jesus didn't say, "You will sin no more." Jesus said, "I don't condemn you. Leave this place of accusation and leave your life of sin." Jesus was saying, "Go and change yourself." We don't know if this woman was a prostitute or someone who was caught in a sexual relationship with her husband's friend. We do know that there were going to have to be significant changes in her life to carry out this instruction from Jesus. If she was a prostitute, she was going to have to find another way to earn a living. If she was involved in a sexual relationship with someone else, she was going to have to break it off and tell her husband. She was in for some drastic changes either way. Since her sin was made public, she couldn't avoid other people knowing what she had done. More than likely, she confronted her sin and started down a path of changing her behavior.

In my case, as I cried out to God to take my addiction away, I wasn't truly facing my sin. I was crying out to God to do the work for me. Each time I cried out to God, I thought I was sorry. In fact, I wasn't expressing

Godly sorrow, I was expressing worldly sorrow. I was crying out, "God fix me without it costing me anything!"

Jesus is enough if we seek him broken and truly repentant. "The sacrifice you desire is a broken spirit. You will not reject a broken and repentant heart, O God" (Psalm 51:17, NLT).

Tim Challies shared a poem written by a woman whose husband had given in to the lure of pornography and became addicted:

"I Looked For Love in Your Eyes."[24]

I saved my best for you.
Other girls may have given themselves away,
But I believed in the dream.
A husband, a wife, united as one forever.

Nervous, first time, needing assurance of your love,
I looked for it in your eyes
Mere inches from mine.
But what I saw made my soul run and hide.

Gone was the tenderness I'd come to know
I saw a stranger, cold and hard
Distant, evil, revolting.
I looked for love in your eyes

And my soul wept.

Who am I that you cannot make love to me?
Why do I feel as if I'm not even here?
I don't matter.
I'm a prop in a filthy play.
Not an object of tender devotion.

Where are you?

Years pass
But the hardness in your eyes does not.
You think I'm cold
But how can I warm to eyes that are making
hate to someone else
Instead of making love to me?

I know where you are.
I've seen the pictures.
I know now what it takes to turn you on.
Women…people like me
Tortured, humiliated, hated, used
Discarded.
Images burned into your brain.
How could you think they would not show in
your eyes?

Did you ever imagine,

The first time you picked up a dirty picture
That you were dooming all intimacy between us
Shipwrecking your marriage
Breaking the heart of a wife you wouldn't meet
for many years?

If it stopped here, I could bear it.
But you brought the evil into our home
And our little boys found it.
Six and eight years old.
I heard them laughing, I found them ogling.

Hands bound, mouth gagged.
Fish eye photo, contorting reality
Distorting the woman into exaggerated breasts.
The haunted eyes, windows of a tormented soul
Warped by the lens into the background,
Because souls don't matter, only bodies do
To men who consume them.

Little boys
My little boys
Laughing and ogling the sexual torture
Of a woman; a woman like me.
Someone like me.
An image burned into their brains.

Will their wives' souls have to run and hide like
mine does?
When does it end?

I can tell you this. It has not ended in your soul.
It has eaten you up. It is cancer.
Do you think you can feed on a diet of hatred
And come out of your locked room to love?

You say the words, but love has no meaning in
your mouth
When hatred rules in your heart.
Your cruelty has eaten up every vestige of the
man
I thought I was marrying.
Did you ever dream it would so consume you
That your wife and children would live in fear
of your rage?

That is what you have become
Feeding your soul on poison.

I've never used porn.
But it has devastated my marriage, my family,
my world.

Was it worth it?[24]

Do you feel the hurt and pain in this poem from this anonymous woman? The suffering she has endured is heartbreaking. Her little boys will surely be impacted by what that man has done.

"And this is the message I proclaim—that the day is coming when God, through Christ Jesus, will judge everyone's secret life" (Romans 2:16, NLT).

Eventually, you will be discovered. God already knows. Your spouse senses that something is wrong. You know what it is. If you are a single man, you have questioned whether your behavior is normal. Does God expect me to be sexually pure? Yes, God wants and expects us to be sexually pure. Sexual purity is possible with the right heart, accountability, and support.

Jesus is enough if you turn to Him with the right attitude and the right kind of sorrow. Jesus will help you along your path of recovery and restoration. Jesus will also help the ones you have hurt. Turn to Him right now and ask Him to show you the condition of your heart. When you see your sin as God sees it, you will be headed in the right direction.

THE POWER OF LUST

There are many powerful struggles that can distract or destroy men. The most powerful of them all is sexual lust. Why is it such a struggle for men to remain pure and holy if we are made in God's image?

The core of the struggle has to do with the God-given desires within our hearts, mixed with a self centered demand for satisfaction, apart from God.

Did God give us sexual desires? The short answer is yes. God is the one who invented sex. God invented sex to create a unifying bond between a husband and wife. If practiced in holy union and according to God's plan, sex between a husband and wife creates an intimate connection that is beautiful and leaves each partner feeling completely fulfilled. If practiced outside of God's plan, this natural, God-designed, intimate act can leave one or both partners feeling frustrated, empty, and alone.

Often a man will act out in completely self-centered and destructive ways, either physically or through an elaborate and intense fantasy world. Many men turn to pornography as a way to sooth their souls, without realizing how damaging and addictive this behavior can become. In today's world, we demand immediate satisfaction. With the accessibility and pervasiveness of provocative images, the Internet, and increased sexualization of our culture, it is all too easy to simply act upon this self-centered desire. "I will have what I want, and I want it now." The more a man turns to *false intimacy* or pixels on a screen, the more his partner is deprived of the true intimacy that God intended for her. Over time, men become desensitized and unable to experience the rewards of a God-designed, truly intimate marriage. Frustration grows, tensions rise, and pretty soon you have two people living together who are not connected at the heart. Do you know couples like this? Is your marriage like this?

As more and more explicit Web sites have become available, the selection of sexual topics has also diversified. It is not unusual for same-gendered sex to be shown on what was once considered a heterosexual Web site. As curiosity is peaked by viewing homosexual acts, many men and women are lured into experimenting with same-sex activities. Mainstream television programming now regularly shows women kissing each other. A growing number of programs promote the gay and lesbian lifestyle. If you have seen any coverage of the Mardi-Gras festival in New Orleans, you know it has become a feast of flashing with bare-breasted women cheered on by a male crowd to make-out in public. This same-sex attraction, for many, is artificially induced by what they are watching. Gaining control of a same-sex attraction is no different than an out-of-control lust for the opposite sex. A person must find ways to refocus their desires to what God has designed for them.

What can you do if your life has been taken over by lust and sexual desires? The first step is to find someone to share your story with. Keeping this deep, dark secret only adds to the power of the struggle. Find someone you trust and tell them what your struggles are. You might be surprised how many men have the same struggles. Once you bring your struggles into the light, find a small group of men, and meet with them on a regular basis. You will need accountability to win this battle. This is one of the most powerful challenges that you will ever face. You cannot do this alone. Being alone is one of the main reasons men struggle.

Are you addicted to something? The American Psychological Association defines addiction as, "the state of being enslaved to a habit or practice or to something that is psychologically or physically habit-forming, to such an extent that its cessation causes severe trauma."

Do you think you might have a sex addiction problem? How do you know if you do? Patrick Carnes, PhD. is one of the world's leading experts on sexual addiction. He lists nine behavior patterns that can be a sign of sexual addiction.

1. Acting out: a pattern of out-of-control sexual behavior.
2. Experiencing severe consequences due to sexual behavior, and an inability to stop despite these adverse consequences.
3. Persistent pursuit of self-destructive behavior.
4. Ongoing desire or effort to limit sexual behavior.
5. Sexual obsession and fantasy as a primary coping strategy.
6. Regularly increasing the amount of sexual experience because the current level of activity is no longer sufficiently satisfying.
7. Severe mood changes related to sexual activity.
8. Inordinate amounts of time spent obtaining sex, being sexual, and recovering from sexual experiences.
9. Neglect of important social, occupational, or recreational activities because of sexual behavior.[25]

If you want more information, visit www.sexhelp.com and take the online "Am I a Sex Addict" screening test. It is free and takes just a few minutes to complete. The test is valid for men or women. If you believe you or family members are addicted, get professional help. There are professionally trained counselors who specialize in this area of addiction. They can help you with a plan and assist you in understanding all of the dynamics of your addiction. If you could have fixed this yourself, you would have already done so.

Controlling lust is one of the most challenging things that a man will ever tackle. As men, we are taught that we can fix anything. This is one thing that most of us will never be able to fix on our own. Left unchecked, sexual addiction is a direct path to destruction and chaos. Becoming pure in heart, soul, and mind is possible if you seek it with a group of supportive, loving, and accepting Christian brothers. Becoming pure requires confession to the Lord and confession to another brother in Christ. "Therefore confess your sins to one another, and pray for each other that you may be healed" (James 5:16).

Healing starts with confession. Recovery starts with being transparent. Purity is a journey. God is willing, able, and ready to help you fight and win this battle. Are you ready to start?

THE POWER OF FANTASY

> "There are some people who live in a dream world, and there are some who face reality; and then there are those who turn one into the other."
>
> —Douglas H. Everett

Pornography, gambling, and drugs are examples of activities that are carried out in a fantasy world. Each promises one more adrenaline rush. Each promises one more experience that will provide happiness or escape from real problems. Porn addicts replace a real woman with a fantasy world where every woman says "yes." Gambling addicts replace financial common sense with the false belief that, *just one more time and I'll beat the odds*, when they know the odds are never in their favor. Drug addicts set everything aside in favor of getting their next *fix*.

What is it that drives so many people to live in a fantasy world instead of reality? For many, reality can be a painful experience. Staying in a committed relationship is really hard work. Marriage is a lifelong commitment that seldom, if ever, goes perfectly. We are all susceptible to being worn down by tension in relationships. The question is: how do we handle the rough times? You know those times when you wonder why you ever got into a relationship in the first place. Maybe it's the latest argument over where to have dinner. Maybe it's the disagreement on how to manage money. There are a thousand other things that can become like compressed springs in a box, just waiting to explode. When they do explode, it's never pretty.

I'm a non-confrontational person. For me, I try to avoid arguments or fights at all costs. Many times I simply shut down instead of calmly discussing my position. Instead of getting the tension out of the way immediately, I tend to let it pile up until I'm the one blowing upThe easy escape route is to live in a fantasy world where there are no arguments, disagreements, or fights. In the short term, we rationalize that we will have peace, contentment, and happiness. For a while, we can live out our dreams in a world free of the bothersome traits of our significant other. The truth is that living in a fantasy world robs us of the opportunity to have real intimacy with another human being. You can never connect in a deep way with a fantasy. In fact, all emotional attachment in a fantasy world is a lie. Believing in something that is not true is the first step to insanity. The fantasy always leaves you feeling like you are missing something. A hole develops that the fantasy cannot fill. Eventually the emptiness becomes so vast that even the fantasies cannot fill them. A vicious cycle develops until you realize that reality is better than fantasy. Every once in a while, your real relationship provides what you need in your emptiness. As time goes by, if you begin to pursue reality, in spite of the risks, you learn that the rewards of being in a real relationship outweigh the perceived benefits of fantasy.

For the addict, there is always a tug back to the dark side of the fantasy world. Your mind will tell you that reality is "too hard—it's not worth the work." But time and effort spent in reality can and will lead to unbelievably deep, personal connections in your relationships. You find out that the other people in your life have some of the same concerns, anxieties, and fears that you do. You find out that you are not alone. There are people who will care about you just the way you are.

Have you been to one of the world famous Disney parks? The first time you attended, were you mesmerized by all of the exhibits and amazing special affects? I remember being at the Epcot Center in Florida when the Michael Jackson 3D film, *Captain EO* debuted. It was so cool and futuristic. We wore these technologically advanced 3D glasses. My little girls were amazed. So was I.

I went back several years later and realized the fantasy for me had worn off. I now understood how all of the special effects were done. I knew about the massive underground complex where all of the workers entered the park in-character. I knew how much money was being made off of the poor sap across the sidewalk with the five kids screaming for more stuff to take home. Reality had sunk in. The fantasy that was Disney had lost its luster for me. Don't get me wrong, it's still a great place for entertainment, but it's a great example of having a perspective of fantasy versus reality being changed.

In what area of your life do you need to have a reality check? Are you living in a world of fantasy propped up by a steady diet of porn? Be careful if you are; the power of porn may be much greater than you think.

THE SCIENCE BEHIND PORNOGRAPHY ADDICTION

The following excerpts are from two expert witnesses testifying before the United States Senate Committee on Commerce, Science, and Transportation, Thursday, November 18, 2004:

> Dr. Judith Reisman (expert witness):
>
> ...Thanks to the latest advances in neuroscience, we now know that pornographic visual images imprint and alter the brain, triggering an instant, involuntary, but lasting, biochemical memory trail... This is true of so-called "soft-core" and "hard-core" pornography. And once new neuro-chemical pathways are established, they are difficult or impossible to delete.
>
> Pornographic images also cause secretion of the body's "fight or flight" sex hormones. This triggers excitatory transmitters and

produces non-rational, involuntary reactions; intense arousal states that overlap sexual lust— now with fear, shame, and/or hostility and violence. Media erotic fantasies become deeply imbedded, commonly coarsening, confusing, motivating and addicting many of those exposed. Pornography triggers myriad kinds of internal, natural drugs that mimic the "high" from a street drug. Addiction to pornography is addiction to what I dub erototoxins — mind-altering drugs produced by the viewer's own brain.

How does this 'brain sabotage' occur? Brain scientists tell us that "in 3/10 of a second a visual image passes from the eye through the brain, and whether or not one wants to, the brain is structurally changed and memories are created – we literally 'grow new brain' with each visual experience."

This scientifically documented neuro-chemical imprinting affects children and teens especially deeply; their still-developing brains process emotions differently, with significantly less rationality and cognition than the adult brain.

Children and others who cannot read will still instantly decode, feel and experience images. Largely right-hemisphere visual and non-speech stimuli enter long-term memory, conscious and unconscious. Any highly excitatory stimuli (whether sexually explicit sex education or X-Rated films) say neurologists, "which lasts half a second within five to ten minutes has produced a structural change that is in some ways as profound as the structural changes one sees in [brain] damage...[and] can...leave a trace that will last for years.[26]

Exposure to pornography can and does alter the brain. Pornography interferes with healthy sexual development in children. Families suffer the consequences of changed behavior. The strength and power of the changes to the brain are astounding and everyone should pay attention to the risks of pornography viewing.

Dr. Mary Anne Layden (expert witness):

Pornography, by its very nature, is an equal opportunity toxin. It damages the viewer, the performer, and the spouses and the children of the viewers and the performers. It is toxic mis-education about sex and relationships. It is more toxic the more you consume, the "harder" the variety you consume and the younger and more vulnerable the consumer.

The executive who goes to his office and logs on to the Internet porn sites at nine a.m. and logs off at five p.m. is out of control and risks a great deal. Research indicates that seventy percent of the hits on Internet sex sites occur between nine to five on business computers. Research also indicates, and my clinical experience supports, that forty percent of sex addicts will lose their spouse, fifty-eight percent will suffer severe financial losses, and twenty-seven to forty percent will lose their job or profession.

Research indicates that even non-sex addicts will show brain reactions on PET scans while viewing pornography similar to cocaine addicts looking at images of people taking cocaine. This material is potent, addictive and permanently implanted in the brain.[27]

When I'm asked how strong sex addiction is, I refer to the brain chemistry. Understanding that my brain had been rewired by the thousands and thousands of images helped me understand the mechanics of my behavior. I began to understand how masturbation and orgasm had been the needle in my arm, reinforcing every sexual act. My brain had been altered to crave the images, the excitement, and the lure of each secret encounter. With each bout of depression, anxiety, frustration, and fear, I would need another *fix* to find internal brain chemical balance.

How strong is this connection in my brain? Think of it this way: each time a person acts upon a sexual impulse or views pornography, a new pathway—or let's call it, a single thread—is created for the neuro-chemicals of pleasure to be released in our brain pleasure center. Masturbation links the thread to the pleasure center. Every time that a similar behavior is repeated, a new thread is added to this tunnel. The old one is still there, but new pathways are constantly added. With every repeated behavior, the bundle of threads builds upon each other and bond together. After days, weeks, and years of repeated behavior, you no longer have a single thread to your pleasure center; you have a tightly wound, extremely strong cable that easily leads you to inappropriate behavior. The worst part of this extremely strong cable is that it is so strong that it overtakes thoughts, feelings, emotions, and rationale. This bundled cable to your pleasure center is almost impossible to break, because it reroutes normal thinking and causes you to be impaired in your thinking.

Understanding the brain chemistry also enlightened me on how to create new healthy pathways that would prevent me from relapsing and repeating the pattern of guilt and shame that I had learned so well. Rewiring your brain is possible!

HOPE, CHALLENGE & FEAR

There is hope for anyone fighting the battle of sexual addiction. Hope starts with finding out that you are not alone and knowing that others have won against the odds of this struggle. Another ray of hope is provided when you gain knowledge about sex addiction. Because so much of the struggle has to do with brain chemistry, there is a really good chance that you can learn to rewire your brain and overcome the situations that cause you to fail.

Jesus Christ also provides us hope:

> No temptation has overtaken you except what is common to mankind. And God is faithful; he will not let you be tempted beyond what you can bear. But when you are tempted, he will also provide a way out so that you can endure it.
>
> 1 Corinthians 10:13 (NIV)

Many times I didn't think that there was a way out. I know now that the thick fog of addiction had blinded me. The way out was there all along. I just couldn't see it. Remember, temptation is not sin; acting on the temptation is sin. Jesus was tempted, but never acted on the temptation. Don't you wish we could be that strong? We can be strong if we have our eyes, mind, and heart wide open to the truth about how to defeat this terrible addiction.

Here's another story from a dear friend who has traveled a similar path to my own. Brett is the founder of Changing Lanes ministry. His story will show you that there is hope for all of us. Visit his Web site at: changinglanesministries.com

> At the age of eight years old, I was exposed to the *Playboy* Channel in my home. The rest of my years growing up, pornography was a part of my life. At the end of my sixth grade year, I was allowed to have cable TV and HBO in my room for doing well on my report card. The ability to hide in my room and view the soft pornography filled the curiosity in my mind about women. It was a part of my life that I hid from all around me. It was something I was embarrassed to admit I enjoyed. My high school and early college years were filled with times of trying to stop viewing pornography. While in the middle of trying to find out how I should live my life as a male with a secret, I accepted Christ as my Lord. But there was not a true repentance for the secret I kept hidden from all around me.

At the age of twenty-one, I married my beautiful bride, Christi. Early on in marriage, I tried to avoid porn. Each time ended in failure. I felt that I was alone. Ashamed and fearful to lose everything, I kept my secret to myself. Each year that I kept the secret alive, I dug deeper into the realm of sexual addiction: pornography Web sites, cyber chatting, chatting on the phone, to meeting someone. Each time things escalated and I indulged in the sinful act, I would go to God and ask for forgiveness, "It's me and God, we can work this out." Never did I see a change in my heart. It only continued to get worse as I ended up meeting more women. In my selfish desire for change, I forgot a few small things required to overcome the addictions and find grace. Finally at the age of thirty, through a trio of events prompted by God, my eyes were opened to the need to confess my addiction. Through some prompting from God, I confessed to my wife and my men's small group. Everyone offered their love and support. The confession gave me a relief and a removal of the burden of secrecy.

Jumping ahead two years, God again gave me a prompting to share my story with others. In October of 2006, I shared my story with my Sunday school class. Six months later, He prompted me several times to share with our church. Christi and I shared our story with Liberty Church in Broken Arrow, Oklahoma, on June 3, 2007. Within a few hours of speaking to the church, God laid on my heart a desire to help others.

Since the fall of 2007, I have been meeting with men on a 1-on-1 basis to help them find victory over sexual addictions. Continuing the path of obedience, I have launched Changing Lanes to give men a place to find hope through one on one mentoring. Now I look forward to seeing where He takes me from here!

While we are speaking of challenges, let me share this analogy. I believe men need to be challenged. If you played little league or high school football, you know that coaches yelling at players is a given. Coaches are going to yell about everything. Coaches are going to make you run when you or one of your distracted teammates is goofing off. Let's say your position is an offensive lineman. The line coach has spent eight weeks teaching you the proper techniques to protect your quarterback on a pass play. The coach blows the whistle, the play begins, and your blocking assignment blows right past you and viciously sacks the star quarterback for a twelve-yard loss. What is the coach likely to do? Is he going to politely walk up to you and say, "Pretty please with sugar on top, would you do a better job next time?" No, he's probably going to grab your facemask, get in your face, and let you know that if that ever happens again, you'll be sitting on the bench the rest of your life, minding the water bucket. As men, how do we react to this *in our face* challenge? Do we run home to mommy and complain about the big, bad coach? No, we take it like a man and then make sure we park that defender on his blessed assurance the next time he tries to cross the line. We'll die defending that quarterback, even though he gets all the girls.

Outside of sports and maybe work, where do we challenge each other? Where do we rise up to a great cause and say, "Don't cross this line"?

Here's my challenge to you: make that line sexual purity. Challenge yourself and two other men. You need it, and they might just need it more than you. Great causes have great success when ordinary men are challenged to greatness.

The biggest challenge for an addict is also their biggest fear: relapse. Relapse is every addict's worst nightmare. We're not talking about a slip: a brief period of failing then getting back on track. Relapse is going back to the old patterns of behavior and staying there.

Relapse can be caused by a number of things, but it is usually associated with the inability to process fears, pain, hurt, or emotions in a healthy way. Almost all addicts are numbing or avoiding pain in some form or fashion. This can be an emotional hurt or a physical hurt. In my case, I was stuffing my emotions from the pain of having an abusive father. It wasn't only the abuse that caused me to turn to my addiction for comfort, it was also the loss of a normal childhood. When I was a young boy, I couldn't have friends stay the night. I never knew what my father was going to do. My relationships with other kids were shallow at best. All of this avoidance of significant relationships manifested itself in isolation. When I found my father's stash, it fit very well into my isolationist world. I didn't need friends; I had my porn.

When a person enters recovery, their relapse triggers are still present. As a person begins the healing process, they learn what their triggers are and how to handle them when their triggers scream out to them to act out through their addiction.

The greater hope is that with prayer, support, and counseling, these triggers simply become annoyances rather than the lightning rods that start you down the path of behavior you don't want to do.

WINNING STRATEGIES

With everything you've read so far, you may be asking, "Okay, how do I get out of this cycle of bad behavior?" The keys are confession, accountability, and finding the right kind of help from the right kind of people.

Confession

Confession to another human being is often the first step to recovery. I had confessed my addiction and frustration to God a million times. I had lain sprawled with my face on the floor, weeping and crying out to God to remove this terrible sin from me, only to hear silence in return. There would be brief times that I would not delve into my sexual fantasies. At the most, I might stay *clean* for a few weeks. It always came back.

I wondered if there was something drastically wrong with my character. I wondered if I was mentally ill. Why couldn't I just stop? The guilt and shame were heavier than a fully loaded semi-truck. I was suffocating from the anxiety and fear of being discovered. I was alone in my frustration. No one was talking about this kind of problem. What could I do?

As I recalled in an earlier chapter, I finally told someone. This simple act, while terrifying, was the most freeing moment in my life. In my case, the first person I told my deep, dark secret was my wife. Understand I was so despondent about my inability to defeat this addiction; I was prepared to lose my wife. I was prepared to never see my two daughters again. I expected to never be able to see my grandchildren again. Even with these possibilities, I was ready to end the most well-guarded secret of my life. I couldn't hold it in any longer. While it was the worst day of my life (and my wife's), it was also the best day of my life. This was the day that God showed himself to be real. I had read James 5:16 many times in my life as a Christian, but I never understood what it meant.

"Therefore confess your sins to each other and pray for each other so that you may be healed. The prayer of a righteous person is powerful and effective" (James 5:16, NIV).

In this rarely understood verse, James expresses a truth about Christian fellowship. God wants us to confess our sins to each other. Wow, I know what you are thinking: *I'm not going to be the first in line for this public sin dumping*. If you've been in church very long, you know that Christians tend to practice cannibalism and eat their own. Most of us cannot imagine being in a church service where everyone confesses their deep, dark, sinful secrets. That is not what I believe it means. It does mean to share your sins and struggles with another trusted Christian. This is the path to healing. Freedom begins with transparency and learning to share your feelings. Freedom comes when Satan can't beat you up about your secrets. Temptation begins to evaporate when someone else knows who you really are inside.

Let me warn you also that you must be extremely cautious about who you share your struggles with. Not every Christian is mature enough to handle confidential information. As a matter of fact, very few Christians handle private information as it should be handled. Finding the right person takes prayer and perhaps years of relationship building. This is no small or inconsequential step. I believe it is one of the most important commandments in the Bible. Every Christian should be in close enough fellowship with one other believer to be able to share anything with them and still be loved and accepted. After all, who can cast the first stone?

It is no accident that the second sentence in James 5:16 refers to the "prayer of a righteous person." If sinful people are confessing their sins to each other, aren't they both sinful? Yes, they are. But healing follows confession. After healing comes righteousness, and after righteousness comes powerful and effective prayer. It all starts with confession. It is not only confession to God; it is also confession to one other trusted believer.

If you have never confessed your sins to another person, find a practicing Catholic. Ask them how they feel after their time of confession with their priest. There is something about telling another human being your struggles. It is therapeutic. It is comforting. It is healing, just as scripture says.

Confession is the first and most important step to recovery in any addiction. A person must recognize that they have a problem and admit it. Every addict has told himself or herself, "I can do this myself." This rarely, if ever works. Confession is the first step, but to make recovery last, you must progress to the next step, accountability.

Accountability

If confession is the first step to recovery, then accountability is the most important step to sobriety. Every person, if left alone with his or her addiction, will fail. I'm not saying that everyone without accountability will fail. I'm saying that there will be many slips and falls on the road to recovery. Sharing how you fell into temptation provides insight on how to overcome your tendencies to repeat your past mistakes.

Support comes in many forms: family, a spouse, counselors, therapists, groups, and clergy. Accountability comes in one form: a close friend who understands the truth about your struggles and is willing to openly hold you accountable for your behavior. Finding that one person who will hold you accountable in the right way can be a challenge and may require many attempts.

My first accountability partner was a complete failure. He showed concern for me, and I truly believe he loved me for the person I was, but he wouldn't share his innermost feelings about anything. An accountability partner is not someone who simply lectures you about everything you confess. A true accountability partner is someone who listens for ways to prevent future problems and guides you to a relationship of mutual trust. Remember, most addicts are loners. Being alone allows for secrets. Secrets destroy recovery.

Prayerfully seeking the right accountability partner is the first step. Without prayer, you will be disappointed. I prayed for a year before my current accountability partner and I were bonded together. We had both been seeking an accountability relationship and had both been praying about it.

Another difficult step is to ask someone to be an accountability partner. You will find yourself avoiding this step. *What if they say no? What if they think I'm weird? What if it doesn't work out? What if they tell someone about my struggles?* All of these thoughts crossed my mind. All of these are thoughts that paralyzed me with fear. At some point I simply had to trust God to allow me to find the right person. And He did! This is something that God wants for every Christian. It's like praying for God to seek out those who He wants to save. God is always seeking out people that He wants to be His children. God will provide you a Christian accountability partner if you ask Him. Don't let fear prevent you from having one completely trustworthy, caring, and loving friend. I can say without hesitation that my accountability partner is one of the dearest friends I have had or will ever have. I believe he would say the same thing about me. There is no other connection like it, except for a spouse.

Speaking of spouses, the worst thing to do is to ask your wife to be your accountability partner. It's not that you don't love your wife, it's that she already carries a heavy enough load. She already knows your struggles and your addictive patterns. As a man who struggles with lust, it doesn't help my wife to hear every thought that crosses my mind in a twenty-four-hour period. Believe me, I do my absolute best at corralling my mind, but if I see some beautiful lady in a revealing outfit walking down a grocery aisle, I can have a fleeting thought that my wife would shoot me for. As long as I don't let this take me down the path of uncontrollable lust, it is better to share this incident with my accountability partner. He can ask me about whether I controlled my mind and my eyes without damaging the progress I've made with my wife over the last days, weeks, months, or years in building back her trust.

Here's another story from someone we'll call Tom:

> This is a not so easy to tell story but I've found that if it helps others to tell it, I will. A man molested me at a very young age. I had not told anybody about this until just two days ago. I told my wife. I guess you could say that this is where my journey began. Did I do something wrong? No, I don't believe so. I was so young I didn't even know what was happening or who to tell if I could. It only happened once, but that was enough. This hasn't really haunted me, but the path I took after the incident has had an impact.

It was around the time of my molestation that I was introduced to pornography. What a thrill! I was eleven or twelve, and it was exhilarating. Of course, you know you're doing something wrong when you have to hide it, but I continued anyway. This evolved, as it became more and more available at the drop of a hat. I tried many times to stop because I knew it was wrong. It was my escape. It was my comfort zone when home life was horrible, which was most of the time.

I didn't have anyone to talk to about it other than young guys going through the same thing and their influences were not good. They were worse than me. This continued on through junior high school where I went from watching it, to experimenting. At the age of fourteen, I got a neighborhood girl pregnant. This crushed me. The response from my parents was devastating. They were very cruel and hateful rather than loving and encouraging. This only pushed me further away.

I had grown up in church though, so I knew the truth. I just chose to go my own way, in complete rebellion to God and His word. Not long after I found out the girl was pregnant, I was told she had an abortion. This killed me. Though I was only fourteen, I knew I had to step up and take care of this girl and the baby we had made. Those thoughts were out the window when I heard of this. As you can imagine, my heart was heavy and my burden was huge. Just try to live life like nothing ever happened after that...it's impossible!

I know now that this was God trying to shake me up a bit and show me that what I was doing was wrong! I listened... somewhat. I was still a male, and still had male urges. I continued to look at pornography after that, though I was too scared to have sex with anyone. Eventually, in high school, I met my future wife. We dated for three years without having sex before we got married. Little did she know, I still had a problem. I thought like many other men did, that it would just go away. It most certainly did not. It got worse!

Finally, after watching the popular Christian movie *Fireproof*, I felt the urge to tell my wife what was wrong. This crushed her heart. For over four years, I had been lying to her, and cheating on her with a computer screen. How empty she felt. I lost all trust she had ever had in me. This was a devastating time, but it got better. I needed to tell her so I could get help. I then told my Pastor, who is also my best friend, and since then, I've been able to talk with many men about it. Don't get me wrong, just talking about it doesn't make it go away. It takes some serious discipline, accountability, reading and knowing God's word, and setting up defenses. Do those things, and you can be free!

It takes a lot of courage for a man to admit another man has molested him. There are many, many men who have been carrying this secret around for years and don't know who they can trust. Trust for them does not seem possible because of the pain and embarrassment.

Many times, molested men will strive to prove their *manhood* by taking advantage of as many women as possible. Often they are extremely aggressive and react in anger over even small things. They tend to suppress emotions and feelings and may turn to alcohol, drugs, or pornography as an escape. If you were molested, find someone you can trust and tell them. You may need to seek professional counseling. You know if this has impacted your life and the people around you.

Closing Windows

No matter what steps you take, confession and accountability being two of the most important, you have to limit your access to situations that cause you problems. I call it closing windows.

If you live in the middle of a metro area, you wouldn't leave your house unlocked and the windows open. If you did, you would expect to come home at the end of the day and find your house ransacked and robbed. Why would you treat the windows of temptation any different? Close the windows and lock them.

It would be crazy for the alcoholic to go to a bar to get a glass of milk. The sights, smells, and lure of just one drink can be too much to handle. Why walk into the den of temptations? Don't go to the bar where you know there is a good chance that you will fail.

Here are some ways of removing the things that can be a problem:

1. If the Internet is a problem, get rid of your computer.

While this is not realistic for most people today, if your computer is what causes you to stumble, why continue to deal with your guilt and shame? If you can eliminate your point of stumbling, get rid of it.

2. Install blocking and accountability software.
    Blocking software filters out offensive images and prevents you from going to objectionable Web sites. While they are not 100 percent perfect, they do protect you most of the time. I also highly recommend accountability software. This software tracks every Web site you visit. A weekly report is sent to your accountability partners, showing any problematic sites. Make sure you make your wife or accountability partner the administrator of the software installation. If you don't, the addict in you will convince you to try and beat the software.

3. Guard your eyes.
    Your eyes will get you in more trouble than a mouse stealing cheese from an unsprung mousetrap. Eliminate TV channels, give your spouse the remote control, and avoid the adult themed restaurants, even if they do have great chicken wings.

    For men, the eyes are the gateway to a variety of challenges. With the eye we can allow things to soak into our souls. The eye is like a funnel, which we use to carefully pour images and scenery into our imagination. Our brains then filter and direct these images into our special brain zones where we can catalogue and critique these images and use them at any moment.

It's been said that our minds are like giant computer storage devices. Men can instantly access any image they've ever seen in milliseconds, process it and transform it into part of our highly stimulated imagination. As a man, I understand this all too well. I can go back in time to my very first sexual experiences and recall with great detail everything that happened. I can recall where it occurred, what the weather was like, and what my surroundings were. How amazing, because I can't remember most of the time what I had for lunch yesterday. The difference? I haven't played images of eating lunch over and over in my mind.

The highly charged images or experiences get played over and over and over and over in my mind. When I let my mind run free, these experiences become the fuel that powers my fantasy experience. Only when I take charge of my thoughts do I have any chance at controlling these images, experiences, and temptations.

"We demolish arguments and every pretension that sets itself up against the knowledge of God, and we take captive every thought to make it obedient to Christ" (2 Corinthians 10:5, NIV).

As a sex addict, I cannot count the number of times I have used my brain's immense storage capacity to pull up images and experiences to feed my desire to please myself. The act of masturbation critically reinforces this behavior. Neuro-chemicals shoot through the body. The heart rate increases, and soon a trance-like state is attained where you lose all sense of time and place. Before you know it, you have spent an hour indulging yourself. Orgasm is the final bond between the images and pleasure. This hour of indulgence trains you for a life of addiction. Images enter the eye, fantasy begins, the body adjusts to the craving of wanting the neuro-chemicals, and pretty soon—if the circumstances allow it—you find yourself engaged in activity you don't want to do. Shame enters your heart and mind, causing a depressed emotional low. Your body then craves something to balance your emotional state and then the cycle begins again. This can happen in a few moments or you may cycle in just a few days. As your body adjusts to the neuro-chemicals, it takes more and more stimulation to achieve the same *high*.

You may begin acting out in other, more risky behaviors. You may try more explicit pornography or acting out in other ways to stimulate yourself. All to get the *high* that you think will satisfy you and make you happy. After all, you say to yourself, "I deserve it," or, "If my wife would just...." After every episode of going deeper, you feel shame and embarrassment. You say to yourself again, "That's the last time," yet you haven't been able to stop. It all starts with the eyes.

By allowing your eyes to drink in that *hot-babe*, you are setting yourself up for a physical reaction that you may not be able to control later. The thought of controlling the eyes may seem absolutely foreign to most men. Society surrounds men and women with provocative and seductive images. Is there anywhere you can go today and not be bombarded? Even in churches, women unknowingly dress in ways that can trigger sinful thoughts in men's minds. Watch any television channel, and you can find a smorgasbord of sexual innuendo or activity. Have you wondered why it continues to get more provocative and risqué? The cycle of addiction causes us to need more stimulation to get the same reaction. Hence, more skin and sex are headed our way in all media forms.

You may be thinking it is impossible to simply close my eyes twenty-four hours a day, seven days a week to avoid the temptations. No, I don't expect you to live in a cocoon the rest of your life. If you want to have success corralling your mind, though, it must start with your eyes. You must avoid letting your eyes control your thoughts. If you see a woman that will cause you trouble, immediately look away! In the beginning it will seem impossible, but as you practice this daily, you will begin to notice a dramatic difference. If your girlfriend, fiancé, or wife knows your struggle, they can be a great help. When my wife and I go out to eat at a restaurant, we have an agreed upon strategy. If a beautiful, appealing woman is in my line of site, my wife and I trade spots or we ask for another table. Seems kind of weird doesn't it? But it works. It has been one of the most successful tools I have adopted. It's not foolproof, however. There will be times when you have to have direct contact with some amazingly gorgeous lady. This is when you have to use the second technique, corralling your mind. If your mind starts to wander and fantasize, you have to immediately gain control and force another thought into your mind. This takes practice as well but the more you try, the more success you will have. Keep in mind that your body has been trained to do whatever it takes to stimulate your brain.

4. Get help
   You know if you need help. If you have tried over and over again to gain control over your behavior, and you simply cannot overcome your struggles, you need help. If you could have fixed it on your own, you would have done so by now.

Getting Help; Therapy, and Counseling

My biggest challenge in deciding whether to seek counseling or therapy was convincing myself that it was okay. In plain language, I didn't want to admit that I needed a *shrink*. I don't use that term to insult professional therapists and counselors. I use it to illustrate my apprehension and embarrassment in considering getting help.

I had plenty of excuses. "I can figure this out on my own" (That hadn't worked out before, but that's the lie the addict inside me was telling me). "It's too expensive." "What will my family and friends think if they find out?" I must have come up with at least fifty reasons not to seek help. As we discussed in the research, I was also fighting my religious reasons. "God can fix me if He wants to." "If I just get closer to God and pray more, I'll overcome this." All of these were just excuses not to seek the help I needed.

There are professionals who are specifically trained in the field of sex addiction. The certification is CSAT, or Certified Sexual Addiction Therapist. I strongly recommend that you seek out someone who is trained and certified in this field or find a Christian counselor who is experienced and trained in dealing with sexual addiction.

The first recommendation I received was to visit a Christian counselor. I called and scheduled a counseling session for me and my wife very close to the time of my confession. My wife and I met with him for an hour to review our situation. After a few minutes of telling my story and telling the counselor about how I had confessed my behavior to my wife and pastor, he started talking. He talked and talked and talked. I spent about ten to twelve minutes telling my story. He talked for forty-eight to fifty minutes. At the end of the one-hour session, he said that we were going to be okay and that we didn't need to schedule any further sessions. My wife and I walked out of his office, got into our car, sat there, and said the same thing, "We're not okay!"

Maybe he was not the best Christian counselor. Maybe he had all of the clients he could handle. I'm sure if we had gone to another Christian counselor, we would have probably had a different experience. At the time, I didn't know a good Christian counselor from a hole in the wall. Unfortunately, this Christian counselor didn't know a sex addict from a chocoholic.

I don't want to leave the impression that Christian counselors aren't effective. There are many great Christian counselors that can provide life-changing assistance. Make sure you ask the right questions about their training and experience before you commit to a lengthy counseling plan with any counselor or therapist.

Several months later I found a CSAT, Certified Sexual Addiction Therapist, and the experience has been phenomenal. Choosing an experienced counselor truly makes a difference.

Sexual addiction is a process addiction. Process addictions include sex, relationships, and eating disorders. Basically, these addictions include things that you are not designed to live without. A person can live without cocaine. A person can live without alcohol. The bulimic or anorexic person struggles with food. They will always struggle with food, because they have to eat food to survive. The sex addict will always struggle with healthy sexuality, because we are designed to have sex in a committed relationship. Sex is part of our biological makeup. Men's bodies are designed for a release of sperm every seventy-two hours.

I explain the challenge of process addictions this way: the person in recovery for cocaine addiction doesn't walk into a grocery store and see cocaine on the shelf. The food or sex addict walks into the grocery store and sees a menu of temptation. For the food addict, it is the variety of ice creams, snack cakes, or other tempting foods. For the sex addict it is the magazine racks that have scantily clad women and provocative titles. For the sex addict, it might be the clerk with the low cut blouse or the knockout woman who keeps crossing your path as you go up and down the aisles.

Process addictions are some of the hardest addictions to overcome. Professional help may be the only way to overcome your addiction and begin the long road to recovery.

Porn Sunday Services

Pastors and clergy are faced with many challenging topics in today's culture. Pornography and sexual dysfunction are two of the toughest.

These are the typical responses I get when I bring up the topic with pastors:

1. "This is not a problem in my church." (Denial)
2. "We have some people struggling with pornography, but the word of God can set them free. If they would just get right with God, they

will be okay." (True, but somewhat of a "head-in-the-sand" approach.)

3. "We've already addressed this topic." (As if to say, it has been fixed.)
4. "We have a growing problem, but I don't know what to do." (Waiting for spiritual enlightenment.)

Please understand I know that pastors and clergy face a multitude of difficult situations: unrepentant churchgoers, undedicated followers, troublemakers, gossips, and more. Few people understand the daily challenges and unreal expectations that church members and attendees place on their pastors. They are expected to have every answer for every situation that could ever arise. They are expected to have a list of talents and abilities second only to Jesus himself. Pastors are expected to walk on water and not sink, like Peter.

My heart's desire is to help pastors and clergy with the most challenging topic of our time. Simply avoiding sexual sin as a topic will not solve what it is doing to the church. Churches are becoming less and less effective because of our sexually immoral activities and lack of sexual purity. Statistically, like divorce, the church is no different than society when it comes to sexual immorality. Referring to the research in the previous chapter, the church is at greater risk of sexual sin than our non-Christian counterparts. The church's lack of teaching regarding healthy human sexuality creates an environment where Christians are less likely to seek help if they have a problem.

The one thing God has given me clear direction on in my journey is starting to talk about sex addiction. If I could have chosen my life's calling in ministry, I assure you that it wouldn't have been on the topic of sex addiction. But since it is, how do we get the church to start talking about sex addiction?

When I first speak to a pastor, I usually start with my story. If they don't pass out from shock, I ask this simple question: "If you had fifty percent of your men and twenty percent of your women addicted to cocaine, what would you do about it?" I let the silence linger for a few moments and wait for their reply. They usually start talking about meeting with their deacons or elders to develop a plan. Then they describe how they would offer counseling and tailor their messages to help those in need. They would offer financial assistance to those who need professional counseling. They will list a host of ways they would be helping their members. I then simply say, "You have fifty percent of your men and twenty percent of your women who are involved in sexual sin, either through the Internet or through flirtatious relationships, so what is your plan to help them before they destroy themselves and their families?"

If you doubt me, have the courage to survey your congregation. There is a right way and a wrong way to do this. Before you survey your members, give me a call or check out the Web site at www.menlivingup.org. If done correctly, you will be amazed at the survey results. Not only will surveying open your eyes, it will provide you a great way to introduce the topic of sexual sin, especially if you are part of the estimated 40 percent of clergy who struggle as well.

A Porn Sunday Service is a great way to start the discussion. God seems to be moving more and more churches to conduct a Porn Sunday service. While I am extremely excited and thankful that churches are finally recognizing the need to start talking about the destructiveness and influence that pornography is having in our churches and our society, there are definitely some *best practices* that should be carefully considered. The main consideration is what to do on the Monday after your very first Porn Sunday.

One of our directors at Men Living Up, Inc. is constantly reminding us of what Matthew 12: 43-45, says:

> When an evil spirit comes out of a man, it goes through arid places seeking rest and does not find it. Then it says, "I will return to the house I left." When it arrives, it finds the house unoccupied, swept clean and put in order. Then it goes and takes with it seven other spirits more wicked than itself, and they go in and live there. And the final condition of that man is worse than the first. That is how it will be with this wicked generation.
>
> Matthew 12: 43-45 (NIV)

Bringing the topic of pornography into the light is telling Satan that you are ready for a fight! Are you? Are you really prepared for the fight? Are you ready, willing, and able to help individuals and families for the rest of their lives?

You should recognize that this is a long-term battle before you enter the battlefield. This is something that must be taken seriously and with a great deal of preparation and prayer.

Here are some helpful tips to conduct a Porn Sunday Service. You definitely need a long-term strategy to be effective in this battle. Here are some basics:

1. Take time to educate yourself and your team about what is really going on as it relates to the church and pornography use.
2. Make sure your pastor, staff, and leadership are completely behind the Porn Sunday service. This is not a gentle nod because the pastor is willing to do it, but a realization and commitment that this must be addressed together, now, for the future of your church.
3. Make sure you have a team of men and women who are willing to participate in leading a ministry to help men and women who are trapped by this secret sin. No judgmental people allowed; they must love the people right where they are.
4. Spend more time on the weeks after the service than the Porn Sunday service. The key is to have a *safe place* for people to get help.
5. Survey your church. While not every Pastor will be willing to do this, it is a great way to see the problem as it truly is. To get an honest survey, you

have to conduct the survey where everyone will feel that his or her answers will be completely confidential. Here's one way to conduct the survey: at the end of your normal service, ask the ladies to leave the sanctuary so that the men can take the survey. Have them spread out, fill out the survey, and place them in a box where no one can see their answers. Repeat the process the following week by dismissing the men and have the women take the same survey. Don't forget to include your youth, ages sixteen and up. Make sure you have the parents' written permission for anyone under eighteen to participate in the survey. Tally the answers and prepare to share the results on Porn Sunday. There's nothing like hearing your own statistics. If you've conducted the survey right, you'll probably fit pretty close to the national averages.

6. The message for the Porn Sunday service must include the message that there is hope, love, and acceptance for anyone struggling. To be most effective, a testimony or real life story should be a part of the service. People respond to people who have *lived it*!

7. Don't ask or expect people to confess their secret sin in the public service. Provide safe small groups within a week of the service during which the facilitators begin the process by telling their own stories. You might even create a submission form on your Web site where people can anonymously share their story.

8. Create continuity. This will be a lifelong struggle for many men and women. Don't treat this as another bullet point on a list of things to cover. This ministry must continue for as long as people breathe. Again, if this scares you, don't start!

9. Tell the stories! As men and women are freed from their bondage, encourage them to share their stories. Be sure to always get written permission before you share their story, especially if you are going to use their real names. In most cases you should keep their names protected. They can either write them out and submit them anonymously, or for the ones who have the freedom and permission from their spouse, they can share their story in future, follow-up Porn Sunday services. The stories motivate others to seek help. The realization that other people have some of the same problems encourages people who are struggling to seek help. Seeing the church forgive, love, and accept people—in spite of their faults—draws people outside of the church to the church.

My prayer is that more people will have safe places to fight the battle with a group of loving, caring people.

There are people in your church, struggling right now. They are simply waiting to find out they are not alone and that someone will love and accept them in spite of their secret sins.

The groups of people who are the most at risk of sexual addiction are pastors and clergy. Their isolation puts them at a greater risk than most people to become addicted and keep the secrets that destroy them and their ministry.

PORN FOR PASTORS

Pastors and clergy are special breeds. It takes a very special person to teach a group of people to follow Jesus Christ and live according to His commands. It takes a special person to sacrifice so much to share the Gospel of Jesus Christ in a world that seems so intent on not hearing God's message. The challenges for today's pastors are mountainous.

As a pastor, you have a dream of entering ministry to please God and to follow His calling on your life. But first you have to get hired. To get hired you are expected to go to school for half of your adult life to learn everything there is to know about God, the Bible, and how to counsel for every possible situation that could ever arise. Next, you are expected to serve in some entry-level position on a church staff and pay your dues at almost poverty level wages. All the while, you have to execute your assigned ministry duties with absolutely no flaws or missteps. After you faithfully serve and endure deacons, elders, panhandlers, church directory salesmen, and Mrs. Always-Right-And-You're-Wrong, who sits in pew number two, because she is a charter member, then you may be considered for that church pastoral position, where everything is all right at the church you are interviewing for. If you are fortunate enough and God answers your prayers, you land your first pastoral job. After one month on the job, you realize nothing the pastor's committee told you was true, but the deacons expect you to fix everything in another month. By the way, you're asked if you can do a *tithing* sermon to get the offerings up. Sound familiar? No, I haven't been bugging your office or stealthily observing your church. This same sequence of events happens too many times to count.

On top of everything that you have experienced as a new pastor, you are expected to maintain a positive, uplifting spirit and attitude for the entire congregation. If, by accident, you hit your thumb with a hammer, you are expected to quote scripture and not let a stream of curse words come pouring out of your mouth. Your wife is ready to pack up and leave the ministry, and you have just started. What's a pastor to do?

Unfortunately, we as church members and attendees have forgotten that pastors are people, too. We tend to put pastors up on a pedestal and think that they must be holier than everyone else. Just look, we say, "He's been through so much preparation for the ministry. Look at the calling that the Lord has placed on him and his wife." Seminary rarely prepares someone for all of the headaches, trials, and pain that a pastor and his wife endure.

If a pastor has a history of early pornography use, he is just as susceptible as any other man. The added pressure of being held to a higher biblical standard increases the guilt and shame if a pastor struggles with sexual sin.

"Not many of you should become teachers, my fellow believers, because you know that we who teach will be judged more strictly" (James 3:1, NIV).

Confessing an addiction to pornography is about the most fearful thing a pastor can do. Not only does a pastor fear the guilt and shame with his wife and family, but also the ultimate fear is that he will lose his job. This is why very few pastors ever confess their secret life to someone.

We have all seen the headlines of a locally or nationally known pastor who falls through an affair, is caught in a sting for prostitution solicitation, participates in homosexual activity, or solicits an underage boy or girl online. With seemingly no place to turn for help, many pastors struggle to overcome their deep, dark, secret life.

Some denominations are better than others in helping pastors, but almost all denominations ask the pastor to step out of their role for a time. This prevents many struggling pastors from seeking the help they need. I don't condone anyone who is involved in illegal activity continuing in their pastoral role. However, if we can create a safe place for pastors to share their sin, we can prevent many from delving into deeper and deeper destructive behaviors. These addictive behaviors, if confronted early, can be overcome before they become out of control. Pastors who are willing to admit their sin of lust should be allowed to keep their position if they are willing to be accountable and change their behavior. Again, I'm not saying that a pastor who is deeply addicted to sexual sin should be allowed to fill the pulpit on Sunday morning. I am saying that the pastor, who struggles, has Godly sorrow, and repents, should be treated like anyone else who repents and turns away from their sin. Our response to them should be the same response that Jesus gave the woman caught in adultery...

"Go now and leave your life of sin" (John 8:11, NIV).

Our problem as Christians is that we tend to categorize sins. Every sin is rebellion to God. God cannot look upon sin, so which sin disqualifies a pastor? Every one of us is incapable of not sinning as long as we take breath on this earth. God uses imperfect people to do His perfect work.

Pastors need to know that sexual sin is no different than any other sin. Yes, I know pastors understand this, but an environment has been created that elevates sexual sin above all others. If you need convincing that God will forgive sexual sin, just look at King David. In 2 Samuel 11, we find David lusting after Bathsheba. David sleeps with her and has her husband, Uriah, killed. Bathsheba has David's child who later dies, because God was so displeased with David. In a short time, Nathan confronts David, and David repents. While David later paid even more consequences for his sin, God forgave David.

> Then David confessed to Nathan, "I have sinned against the Lord." Nathan replied, "Yes, but the

Lord has forgiven you, and you won't die for
this sin. Nevertheless, because you have shown
utter contempt for the Lord by doing this, your
child will die.

2 Samuel 12: 13, 14 (NIV)

Later David and Bathsheba had another son,
Solomon, who became king. In spite of God's
forgiveness of David, David endured many years of
misery in his kingdom and his family. Trouble followed
him for many years. There are consequences for our sin.

The ultimate ending of David's story is that God
still used him in a mighty way. David is described as
a "man after God's own heart." God used the same
man who lusted, fornicated, murdered, and lied about
it after his terrible sin. Did God disqualify him from
ever being used? No, God used David as the seed for
his own son, Jesus.

If you are a pastor who is struggling with sexual sin,
pornography, or other addictive behaviors, I pray that
you will follow the same steps we've recommended for
every other man. Confess your sin to one other believer.
Find an accountability relationship, and then change
your behavior. If you need professional help, get it
before you do something that costs you everything.

There are some safe places to confess your sin. One
of those places is the Men Living Up blog. There is a
Pastor's Corner, where you can share your story or your
struggles. Visit blog.menlivingup.org. Like every other
man who struggles, the greatest weapon against sin is
to bring the secret sin into the light. The temptation
evaporates when you tell someone. Don't let Satan

defeat you and diminish the impact of your ministry. Return the power of the Holy Spirit to your ministry and your church by traveling the path to sexual purity. God loves you right where you are. Your way of escape is to share your secret with a trusted believer.

If you can't find anyone, e-mail or call me. I would be honored to help you start down the path to sexual purity. You will be amazed how God will empower you to lead your congregation to a new and exciting place of revival.

HOPE FOR FUTURE GENERATIONS

America's hope for future generations lies with you. If you are reading this book, you either know someone who is struggling or you struggle yourself. Perhaps, the title of this book caught your eye, because you discovered a stash a long time ago, and it also had an affect on you. A friend might have given you a copy of this book or recommended it. Maybe you have realized what is happening in our society, and you are concerned. Our children need protection. You wouldn't think of leaving your children with a total stranger, but the vast majority of American families allow their children full, unfiltered access to the Internet. Internet pornographers are looking for any open door to trap their next addict. Maybe you are the one who is trapped. I pray that it won't be your son or daughter who gives in to temptation. Are you ready to protect yourself and your family? It's time to start.

Future generations can only hope that one person at a time will decide to fight against the struggle. Future generations are impacted by our current behaviors and failures. Will you allow the next generation in your family to fall into the same pit of secrets, shame, and guilt? This battle is won, one person at a time.

As you fight and have some victory, you will gain strength. As you gain strength, I pray that you will be willing to share your story—if not with others, then with the closest ones in your family or with one other Christian brother. Your sons and daughters need to know the truth of their adversary's strength. You wouldn't go on the battlefield without knowing everything about your enemy. Your enemy is Satan. He has a clear plan and purpose for your destruction.

> Be alert and of sober mind. Your enemy the devil prowls around like a roaring lion looking for someone to devour. Resist him, standing firm in the faith, because you know that the family of believers throughout the world is undergoing the same kind of sufferings.
>
> 1 Peter 5:8;9 (NIV)

If you apply this verse to today's world, is pornography the tool that Satan has chosen to defeat Christians? Does Satan use the Internet to keep Christians beaten down and ineffective? I see clear evidence that the church is less effective today than it has ever been in America. Why won't we as Christians take a stand? I believe it's because we are deep in our sin. Why don't more men and women confess their sin of lust and turn away from it? The short answer is that we love our sin. I've seen hundreds of men realize that they need to change, recognize that they are not alone in the struggle, and then are never heard from again. When it comes down to fighting the battle or fleeing, most men will flee to the comfort of their sin.

There will be a few men, women, and pastors who experience true freedom and repentance. There will be a few who will understand that they are the only line of defense for their family, marriage, and children. Only a few will dedicate themselves to changing future generations. Only a select few will share their story to change the world. Are you one of the few?

Share your story confidentially by emailing:

stories@menlivingup.org or by using the web submission form at: *http://menlivingup.org/ssl/submit_story.html*

THE SILENCE IS
DEAFENING

So what is next for our society? Some have said that America is training the next generation of rapists and child molesters. It can be frightening to think about how men and women are being impacted by the explosion of free, always available access to more and more explicit and violent images. What does the future hold, and what can we do about it today? Where is the hope for you and your children?

In church culture we must begin talking about healthy human sexuality. Churches and their leaders must begin teaching about and talking about sex. Christian men and women must be educated and informed to protect their family. Christian men, women, and clergy must be loved and accepted if they are willing to admit their struggles and are willing to change. I don't know of a church that wouldn't accept and offer help to a drug addict or an alcoholic. In fact, many churches are providing recovery resources for these more *acceptable* addictions.

There is a tremendous generational gap in the discussion of human sexuality. My generation, the baby-boomers, hide behind embarrassment and a lack of education. Television, movies, the Internet, and pornography producers have taught the younger generations their views about human sexuality. The younger generations know more about sex than any other generation before them. They are comfortable talking about sex, unlike previous generations. However, what they have learned about sex is not necessarily healthy or true. In some cases they have witnessed or been a victim of their family's own unhealthy sexual behavior. All of these lessons learned have a slanted and false view. The pornography producers' motivation is to sell more of whatever they are marketing. Truth has little to do with what they promote. They strive to get more people to watch what they sell. Pornography producers understand all too well how the addictive cycle works. They understand that they have to constantly raise the bar of excitement and mystery to continue maintaining and growing their audience. They understand that what excited someone yesterday won't even interest them tomorrow.

It has been my observation that the church has become silent because the people in the church are just as trapped as the rest of society. How can you fight a battle when you are on the wrong team? How can you speak up when you know you are a hypocrite for speaking out? How can a member of the clergy preach about sexual purity when he has spent more time viewing pornography than preparing his sermon?

It will take men and women of courage to face their own struggles and addictive behaviors to change things. It is time for men and women of all faiths, or no faith, to learn to be transparent and share their stories. I have seen the power of confession and accountability. I have seen men weep as they tell their story and realize that they are not alone. I have seen men of faith become giants of the faith, because they truly followed scripture and shared their secret sin with one other trusted believer. I have seen lives changed through the truth and power of James 5:16: "Therefore, confess your sins to each other and pray for each other so that you may be healed. The prayer of a righteous person is powerful and effective" (James 5:16, NIV).

As I continue to share my story, I see God using my story to help others. Sometimes the person hearing my story becomes motivated to share his.

I recently met someone who was curious about the ministry of Men Living Up. We scheduled a lunch meeting for him and his accountability partner so that we would have enough time to tell the full story. At our lunch meeting, which lasted two hours, I told them how God has called me to share my story with other men.

One of the things I have experienced consistently is that, when I share my story, the person I am sharing with always shares their story. So far, I haven't met a single guy who doesn't have a story. Maybe God hasn't led me to the person who doesn't struggle, or maybe God is just having me meet the people who do struggle with sexual sin. For whatever reason, guys are telling me their stories. There are so many common threads: early exposure to pornography, difficult family situations, and fatherlessness, to name just a few.

Our lunch meeting came to an end, and the two men were in a mild state of shock. My story mirrored so much of theirs. We committed to staying in touch and checking on each other and left the lunch meeting.

The next day one of the guys (I'll call him Bob), emailed me and shared that he had returned to work, and a young man had approached him and asked him about the meeting. Bob shared that we had talked about the power of lust and sexual addiction. Bob shared with this young man that he had personally struggled with lust and sexual sin for years. Pretty brave fella, right? The young man's face became pale and noticeably drawn. He walked slowly to Bob's office door and shut it. He then proceeded to tell Bob that he had struggled with pornography for years. He was tired of the struggle and wanted to overcome this, but had always failed. He had never told anyone about his struggles. He asked Bob to be his accountability partner right there on the spot. Bob had experienced what we talked about at lunch within an hour of our conversation.

Men are waiting for someone to be first. So much of the Christian *walk* is not about walking at all; it's about opening our mouths. We have to open our mouths when the Holy Spirit is speaking to us. How many opportunities have we missed because we were afraid of how the other person would react? How many lives could have been changed if we had only said what God was leading us to say?

Never had this kind of opportunity? Ask God right now to provide just one opportunity. This is a prayer God loves to answer. Be ready, because it will come when you least expect it, and usually much sooner than you expect. What if Bob had just said that it was a "simple business lunch?" Would this man still be imprisoned and alone in his battle?

Remove that tongue depressor of fear and speak when the Holy Spirit tells you to speak. I don't know where this young man is today, but I am confident that God is helping him overcome his struggles.

Will you be one of the few who seeks God's help in fighting and winning the battle? I will be praying that God provides you the courage to start the fight and that God will place people in your life who will encourage you and hold you up as you start down this path to purity.

It is time to end the silence. There is too much at stake. Will you use your voice, or will you be one of the silent ones? If the Holy Spirit is speaking to you right now, make the choice to tell someone your story. The life you change just might be your own!

REFERENCES

1   Saari, P. "Science and Invention- Why Was the Internet Created?." Accessed October, 19, 2011. http://www.enotes.com/history/q-and-a/why-was-internet-created-288816.

2   The Pew Internet Research, "Fall Tracking Survey." Accessed November 7, 2011. http://www.pewinternet.org/~/ media/Files/Questionnaire/2010/PIP_Chronic_Disease percent20_Dec08_topline.pdf .

3   "Internet Access and Usage in the U.S.." Accessed November 7, 2011. http://www.infoplease.com/ipa/A0908398.html

4   Goldsborough, Reid. 2008. "the Internet these days." *Teacher Librarian* 35, no. 3: 72.

5   Baumann, M. "Pew Internet: highlights of the digital domain." *Information Today* 27, no. 4 (April 2010): 13. *CINAHL Plus with Full Text*, EBSCO*host*.

6   Horrigan, J. Pew Internet & American Life, "Seeding the Cloud: What mobile access means for usage patterns and online content." Last modified

March 2008. http://www.pewinternet.org/Reports/2008/Seeding-The-Cloud-What-Mobile-Access-Means-for-Usage-Patterns-and-Online-Content/Seeding-the-Cloud.aspx.

[7] Grant, Jon E, Marc N Potenza, Aviv Weinstein, and David A Gorelick. 2010. "Introduction to behavioral addictions." *The American Journal Of Drug And Alcohol Abuse* 36, no. 5: 233-241. *MEDLINE*, EBSCO*host*.

[8] Sellman, D. 2010. "The 10 most important things known about addiction." *Addiction* 105, no. 1: 6-13. *CINAHL Plus with Full Text*, EBSCO*host*.

[9] Weinstein, A., & Lejoyeux, M.. "Internet Addiction or Excessive Internet Use." *American Journal of Drug & Alcohol Abuse.* 36. no. 5 (2010): 277-283.

[10] Mitchell, K. J., Sabina, C., Finkelhor, D., & Wells, M.. "Index of Problematic Online Experiences: Item Characteristics and Correlation with Negative Symptomatology." *Cyberpsychology & Behavior.* 12. no. 6 (2009): 707-711. doi:10.1089/cpb.2008.0317

[11] Internet Filtering Learning Center, "Pornography Statistics." Accessed November 7, 2011. http://internet-filter-review.toptenreviews.com/internet-pornography-statistics.html.

[12] Preston, Cheryl B. 2008. "INTERnet PORN, ICANN, AND FAMILIES: A CALL TO ACTION." *Journal Of Internet Law* 12, no. 4: 3-15. *Business Source Premier*, EBSCO*host*.

[13] Twohig, MP, JM Crosby, and JM Cox. 2009. "Viewing Internet pornography: for whom is it problematic, how, and why?." *Sexual Addiction &*

Compulsivity 16, no. 4: 253-266. *CINAHL Plus with Full Text*, EBSCO*host*.

14 Bachman, Jerald G., Patrick M. O'Malley, John E. Schulenberg, Lloyd D. Johnston, Alison L. Bryant, and Alicia C. Merline. 2002. *The decline of substance use in young adulthood: Changes in social activities, roles, and beliefs.* Mahwah, NJ US: Lawrence Erlbaum Associates Publishers, 2002. *PsycINFO*, EBSCO*host*.

15 Baltazar, Alina, Herbert W. Helm Jr., Duane Mcbride, Gary Hopkins, and John V. Stevens Jr. 2010. "INTERNET PORNOGRAPHY USE IN THE CONTEXT OF EXTERNAL AND INTERNAL RELIGIOSITY." *Journal Of Psychology & Theology* 38, no. 1: 32-40. *Academic Search Premier*, EBSCO*host*.

16 White, Mark A., and Thomas G. Kimball. 2009. "Attributes of Christian Couples with a Sexual Addiction to Internet Pornography." *Journal Of Psychology & Christianity* 28, no. 4: 350-359. *Academic Search Premier*, EBSCO*host*.

17 Manning, JC. 2006. "The impact of Internet pornography on marriage and the family: a review of the research." *Sexual Addiction & Compulsivity* 13, no. 2-3: 131-165. *CINAHL Plus with Full Text*, EBSCO*host*.

18 Gavish, Bezalel, and Christopher L. Tucci. 2008. "REDUCING INTERNET AUCTION FRAUD." *Communications Of The ACM* 51, no. 5: 89-97. *Business Source Premier*, EBSCO*host*.

19   Burkhalter, C, and J Crittenden. 2009. "Professional
      identity theft: what is it? How are we contributing
      to it? What can we do to stop it?." *Contemporary
      Issues In Communication Science & Disorders* 36,
      89-94. *CINAHL Plus with Full Text*, EBSCO*host*.

20   IRENE LAI KUEN, WONG. 2010. "INTERnet
      GAMBLING: A SCHOOL-BASED SURVEY
      AMONG MACAU STUDENTS." *Social Behavior
      & Personality: An International Journal* 38, no. 3:
      365-371. *Academic Search Premier*, EBSCO*host*.

21   SHAFFER, HOWARD J., ALLYSON J.
      PELLER, DEBI A. LAPLANTE, SARAH E.
      NELSON, and RICHARD A. LABRIE. 2010.
      "Toward a paradigm shift in Internet gambling
      research: From opinion and self-report to actual
      behavior." *Addiction Research & Theory* 18, no. 3:
      270-283. *Academic Search Premier*, EBSCO*host*.

22   Siemens, Jennifer Christie, and Steven W Kopp.
      2011. "The Influence of Online Gambling
      Environments on Self-Control." *Journal Of Public
      Policy & Marketing* 30, no. 2: 279-293. *Business
      Source Premier*, EBSCO*host*.

23   Ropelato, Jerry. ContentWatch, Inc., http://www.
      strengthenthefamily.net/tricks_pornographers.
      php.

24   Anonymous, First. challies.
      com, "http://www.challies.com/
      quotes/i-looked-for-love-in-your-eyes."

25   Carnes, Ph.D., Patrick J. International Institute
      for Trauma & Addiction Professionals, "Sexual

Addiction Screening Test (SAST)." http://www.
sexhelp.com/am-i-a-sex-addict/sex-addiction-test.

26 Reisman, Ph.D., Judith. "The Science Behind
Pornography Addiction." November 18, 2004.

27 Layden, Ph.D., Mary Anne. "The Science Behind
Pornography Addiction." November 18, 2004.

RESOURCES

Men Living Up Magazine

The quarterly issue of *Men Living Up* is a great resource to reach other men in your community.

- Articles and stories to help you in trying to *live up.*
- Lessons, articles, and stories for men who want to be strong and courageous for themselves and their families.
- Help in raising sons and daughters fight the battles that they will face.
- Designed to help future generations face the challenges in today's society.

Men Living Up Workshops

- Learn how to launch an effective men's ministry that tackles today's most relevant issues for men: marriage, work, relationships, addictions to pornography, gambling, and more.

- Educate yourself on today's most challenging topics and receive tools and ministry outlines that can help men build real and relevant relationships with other men.
- Experience accountability group building techniques that will change men's lives.
- Take home tools for changing current and future generations of men.
- Receive a special discount on Internet screening and accountability software

For more information, or to schedule a workshop e-mail: *booking@menlivingup.org*

Porn for Pastors Workshop:

Learn how to address the most challenging issue of our time, pornography and sexual sin. Today's Christian men and women are drowning in shame and guilt. Pornography is destroying men, women, families, and many churches. It's time to face the challenge, strengthen your church, and teach men and women how to defeat this worldwide epidemic.

Need a speaker for your next men's event? Pastor, business leader, and author Jerry D. Wright is available to come to your next men's event. Jerry can provide hard hitting, timely, and relevant topics that men want to hear about, all from a faith-based, biblical perspective.

Some of the topics include:

- How to conduct a Porn Sunday service
- Today's challenges for men

- Building stronger families
- Raising sons & daughters
- Winning the battle against pornography
- Addictions that can destroy your family
- How the church can handle today's *men-only* challenges

Presentations can be tailored to meet your needs. We have one hour to half-day presentations available.

E-mail: booking@menlivingup.org to receive information about fees and availability.

Tell us about your event; estimated attendance, special needs, etc. For more information e-mail: booking@menlivingup.org

Make a tax-exempt donation to:

Men Living Up, Inc.
9309 Lakecrest Drive
Oklahoma City, OK 73159
Men Living Up, Inc. is a 501(c)3 non-profit ministry. All donations are tax deductible.

HOW TO BUILD LASTING ACCOUNTABILITY GROUPS

A n accountability group is a small group of men, usually no more than ten to twelve, who agree to meet on a regular basis to discuss common challenges. These challenges are usually things that the group shares in common.

Purpose of Accountability Groups:

The purpose of accountability groups is to provide a confidential, safe place for men to share their struggles and challenges, and as a group, help each other in successfully improving in their role as men.

Structure:

One or two facilitators normally lead the group. These are people who are willing to be transparent, open, and honest about their own struggles. In addition, they should be skilled at keeping a conversation going.

They should not dominate the group, but enhance every member's participation in the discussion.

Best Practices:
- If you are starting your groups at a church, the two key people are your pastor or clergy and the one man who is driven by a passion to help other men. Without the full support of your pastor or clergy, it will always be a struggle. Without the passion of at least one man called to this purpose, you will not succeed over a long period of time.
- Every member of the group should sign a confidentiality agreement that says that "what is said in the group, stays in the group."
- Meetings should last approximately one hour. Any longer gets to be a burden on family time and work schedules.
- Meetings should occur no less than every other week. Many groups will meet weekly and take two to three week breaks every ten to twelve weeks.
- No judgment allowed. Absolute acceptance of every man, no matter his struggles, is the key to a successful accountability group. The exceptions would be any criminal activity that harms any other person. You should have a reporting mechanism through your church or local officials. When in doubt, speak to a higher authority and ask about it.

- Once a group starts, no additional members can join. Use your own judgment here, but keep in mind that new guys coming in can ruin the trust that has been built among the original members.
- No wife bashing. This is not about how terrible some guy's wife is to him. This is about the man's own issues and how they affect everything in his life.
- Material used for study: any material selected should be relevant and not too complicated. Reading assignments should be short and achievable, according to your meeting schedule.
- Watch out for the dominant member. Every group will tend to have someone who likes to do all the talking; make sure that's not you if you are the facilitator. If someone becomes an issue, talk to them in a kind way after the meeting and make them aware of it. Be sure to stress the importance of every man sharing and talking.
- Don't overreact yourself to those moments when nobody responds to a question. Let the silence hover for a few moments. If you let it go a while, someone usually will add something really valuable to the group.
- Ask guys to become leaders of new groups. New groups are the lifeblood of men becoming involved. Success breeds success. It's easy to become protective and sheltered in your own

little group. However, by protecting yourself in your group you are not reaching other men.

- Have combined meetings of all your groups at least three times a year. The camaraderie and fellowship as a large group feeds the passion and builds momentum. Don't forget that your goal is to reach every man.

- Men and women partners from accountability groups should get together for a social event once or twice a year. This is designed to further connect the group members. If spouses make connections, it is much more likely that men will continue to meet together.

- Accountability groups should lead to one-on-one accountability relationships. This has to be a natural process. You cannot arbitrarily match up guys together. In most cases, a one-on-one relationship will build over time until one man will approach another and ask him to be his accountability partner. They can meet as often as they wish to discuss their own challenges and help each other.

HOW TO SHARE YOUR STORY

As terrifying as it might be, it is important for you to tell your story to other men. There is some risk in sharing your story, so be sure to talk to your pastor or other spiritual leader before you open up to others. Whether you are in recovery from addiction or you are someone who occasionally struggles, it is a great strength builder to share your story with other men. It will strengthen you and give men the opportunity to be free from their deepest, darkest struggles.

If you are a leader or a facilitator of a men's group, you have to tell your story in order to get other men to share their story. You will always have to be first. Men will not open up until they know they are in a safe place and free from worry about having their story spread all over town. It has been my experience that men are dying to tell someone. This is a huge hurdle for every man. In the midst of our struggles, every man feels alone. We learn as young boys that we are to *suck-it-up* and *be a man*. Men also experience deep shame and guilt and tremendous fear in being exposed. If you demonstrate to the men in your group that you trust them by telling your story, then they are much more likely to trust you and tell you their story.

Some key elements:

1. Share your story without all of the explicit details. Tell them enough to let them know what your strongholds have been and how you were captured by your sin. Tell them how you have begun the journey to freedom, yet you still need other men to hold you accountable. Explain to them the truth of James 5:16: "Therefore confess your sins to one another and pray for one another that you may be healed." Bringing our secret sins into the light causes our sins to lose their power over us.
2. Don't try to force a story out of someone. Pray ahead of time that the Holy Spirit will be working in their heart to free them from their captivity.
3. Keep your mouth shut! Confidential means confidential. Nothing will ruin your trust quicker than sharing anything that is shared with you. Again, the only exception is illegal behavior. You have a legal obligation to report this. Check with your leaders or pastor if you are not sure.
4. After you hear their story, offer love, acceptance, and understanding. Pray with them.

Do you have the ability to love someone in spite of his or her sin? Christ loved you in spite of your sin. Love your brother as yourself. When men see other men and accept them in spite of their faults, they truly begin to have hope that they can change their attitude and actions. They also learn how important it is to begin the journey with other men actively involved in their lives.